WILL TORRENT

chocolate
at home

step-by-step recipes to help
you master the art of chocolate

photography by Jonathan Gregson

LONDON · NEW YORK

Senior Designer Megan Smith
Commissioning Editors Céline Hughes and Stephanie Milner
Head of Production Patricia Harrington
Art Director Leslie Harrington
Editorial Director Julia Charles
Publisher Cindy Richards

Recipe Writer and Developer
Annie Rigg
Prop Stylist Jo Harris
Food Stylist Will Torrent
Assistant Food Stylist Emily Kydd
Indexer Hilary Bird

First published in 2014 by
Ryland Peters & Small
20–21 Jockey's Fields,
London WC1R 4BW
and
519 Broadway, 5th Floor,
New York NY 10012
www.rylandpeters.com

Text © Will Torrent 2014

Design and photographs ©
Ryland Peters & Small 2014

ISBN: 978-1-84975-573-3

Printed and bound in China

10 9 8 7 6 5 4 3 2 1

A CIP record for this book is available from the British Library. US Library of Congress Cataloging-in-Publication Data has been applied for.

NOTES
• Both British (Metric) and American (Imperial plus US cups) measurements and ingredients are included in these recipes for your convenience, however it is important to work with one set of measurements and not alternate between the two within a recipe.
• All spoon measurements are level unless otherwise specified.
• All eggs are medium (UK) or large (US), unless specified as large, in which case US extra-large should be used. Uncooked or partially cooked eggs should not be served to the very old, frail, young children, pregnant women or those with compromised immune systems.
• When a recipe calls for the grated zest of citrus fruit, buy unwaxed fruit and wash well before using. If you can only find treated fruit, scrub well in warm soapy water before using.
• Ovens should be preheated to the specified temperatures. We recommend using an oven thermometer. If using a fan-assisted oven, adjust temperatures according to the manufacturer's instructions.
• The moulds used in the testing of the recipes in this book were chosen for specific looks and finishes. Different moulds will yield different quantities of chocolates and truffles and you may need to use more than one mould at a time.

Contents

My history with chocolate

Making chocolates at home is one of my favourite things to do, whether creating simple truffles, tempering wonderful chocolate, baking with it in my Nans' Chocolate fudge cake or just eating it in front of the television – however it comes, I love chocolate!

My love affair with chocolate began as a small child, when I used to bake my favourite cakes with my Nans on my birthday – even now I can remember making the cake batter and icing, decorating cakes with chocolate buttons, scraping out the bowl and licking the spoon. But it was when I was training to be a chef at the University of West London, under the expert guidance of Yolande Stanley MCA, that I really became interested in the dark arts of chocolate making. We covered everything from learning to taste chocolate properly, how to temper it and how to design desserts that used it. Whilst studying I was also in training for the international WorldSkills competition final in Japan and this is where my chocolate training really kicked off. I spent days on end tempering dark/bittersweet, milk/semisweet and white chocolate without using a probe, learning to do it by eye so that I could do it more quickly; piping bulbs of ganache to gauge the correct temperature to pipe at and to improve the consistency in my piping; as well as training with other great chocolatiers including four times winner of Britain's Best Chocolatier, William Curley MCA. With my new found confidence I began to try different brands of chocolate such as Cacao Barry, Valhrona, Amedei, Cluziel and so on, and ended up focussing my dissertation on chocolate!

Years on, I am still in love with all things chocolate and have become passionate about removing the fear factor from making chocolates at home, educating and encouraging people to have a go, not to be frightened by the artistry that is often shrouded in mystery by secretive chocolatiers.

As an international ambassador for Cacao Barry, one of the world's leading chocolate brands, I have, in the last few years, trained my palate by tasting truly wonderful chocolate. And you can do the same. Along the way I have learnt which flavour and textural combinations please the crowds, and what's more, no diner is left behind – many of the ganaches and caramels in this book can be made gluten- and dairy-free by simply replacing cream and butter with fruit purées and olive oil or soy and nut milks.

You're going to need some specialist tools along the way, but these are all worth investing in to help you create chocolate masterpieces that will make you very popular. Whether it's Champagne truffles for a celebration, Cognac, caramel and pear domes for dessert after a posh dinner party or chocolatey Chai macarons for a trendy twist on a French classic, with this book, I hope to guide you through the basic steps that will help you on your way to becoming a chocolatier. You will master the art of tempering, ganache making, moulding and dipping, as well as learn something about the fine art of pâtisserie, using chocolate as an ingredient in desserts, petit fours, ice creams and drinks.

Most of all, I hope you enjoy recreating the recipes in this book at home. And remember a square of good chocolate a day, keeps the doctor away!

Will Torrent

Why do we love chocolate so much?

I love chocolate in many forms: bars, truffles, desserts, drinks – to be honest everything! Over the years as a chocolate lover, my eyes often light up when I see a newspaper article headed 'Chocolate is good for you!' – we are constantly being told by the media that chocolate is, in fact, a healthy foodstuff. So why does it still have such a bad reputation? It seems that the reports contradict themselves. This is because the mass market confectionery that is responsible for giving chocolate a bad name is often low on cocoa and high in sugar and fat. However, good-quality chocolate or 'real' chocolate does have health benefits and when eaten in moderation can have its place in a healthy, balanced diet – well at least that's what I think!

Good chocolate is made from cocoa beans from countries such as Ecuador, Ghana, the Dominican Republic, Tanzania, Cuba and other cocoa growing regions situated between 20° north and 20° south of the Equator. Like fine wine, the taste of cocoa changes from region to region. In wine, this is known as the 'terroir'. While there is no term for this in chocolate, we are starting to see the origins of chocolate bars written on packaging, helping us to better understand the complex, intriguing and interesting flavours that each region has to offer. As a chocolatier, and for you as a chocolate lover, this is where it gets exciting, because like tasting wine, when you select chocolate properly you discover all its different tastes, experiences and feelings.

With 1,500 identified flavours in dark/bittersweet chocolate compared to the 500 found in red wine, chocolate far outnumbers the flavour compounds available to discover in something more widely recognized as a taste experience. As grapes are to wine, the cocoa bean is to chocolate and we need to understand it in this way.

The tongue has five main senses that chocolate can target: sweet, bitter, sour, salt and umami. So with this in mind, how do we really appreciate good chocolate that may cost more than your average bar but will give you a longer lasting, enhanced flavour for more enjoyment, and in smaller amounts? There are a few steps to take to really enjoy and taste chocolate.

Firstly, please don't store it in the fridge. Cocoa butter has a melting point similar to body temperature so chocolate with a good cocoa solids content will melt sharply and cleanly in the mouth. Chilling chocolate takes away from this experience, so store it in a cool, dark place – but not in the spice cupboard, as it can pick up other flavours around it.

Second, open the packet and slowly rip the foil. Chocolate is a multi-sensory experience so use all of your senses when tasting chocolate. We eat with our eyes, so start by looking at the chocolate. It should be glossy, shiny with no visible signs of chocolate bloom. If there is bloom or the chocolate doesn't look very appealing, you may not enjoy the eating experience as much. Smell the chocolate just as you would an expensive glass of wine. There should be wonderfully rich aromas of cocoa, with a degree of smokiness and some roasted notes.

Next, break off a piece. The chocolate, like a musical instrument should make a good sound when it snaps. And finally, pop it on your tongue and allow the chocolate to melt – don't chew it just yet. Your tastebuds will then start to buzz as flavours of dark rich cocoa and sweet vanilla come alive, followed by red berries, vine fruits, spices, pepperiness and sometimes tobacco or deep red wine and port. If you prefer milk/semisweet chocolate, where milk solids and sugar are added during chocolate manufacture, then you could expect flavours such as cooked milk, caramel, rich

double/heavy cream and even sometimes bananas and caramelized nuts.

Once the chocolate has half melted, get your teeth and tongue working to move it around your mouth. Doing this finishes off an amazing taste journey from just one square of chocolate. The chocolate taste should linger in your mouth. Some chocolate will naturally dry your mouth out because of the astringency of the cocoa or depending on how high the cocoa solids content is. It's about recognising different flavour notes and thinking about how you might best show them off in your chocolate tasting, making and baking.

Okay, so how does all this make chocolate healthy? Well, in my book, a little goes a long way but scientists have proven that dark/bittersweet chocolate can be a real benefit to your health. As a natural ingredient cocoa contains flavanols that have antioxidant properties which are proven to be really good for your heart and circulation – chocolate has nearly eight times the amount of antioxidants found in strawberries, blueberries and green tea! Dark/bittersweet chocolate also increases endorphin production – the happy hormone. The recommendation is to eat just under 50 g/2 oz. of dark/bittersweet chocolate a day to make the most of its health benefits, but every now and then why not treat yourself and try a little bit more – it is one of the finest ingredients in the world, so make the most of it!

What chocolate to buy?

Many of the recipes in this book were tested using specific brands of chocolate that I always use and love to work with but there are many producers putting out fantastic chocolate so I've included a list of my favourites in Resources (see page 174). You can buy chocolate in many different bar forms but I tend to buy it in button form as it's easier to weigh out, melt and store – plus there is no chopping involved so it saves on the washing up! Packs of 'real' chocolate buttons are becoming more readily available to buy in supermarkets, food halls and online.

When working with chocolate, and especially when tempering or making a ganache, it is important that you do not buy cooking chocolate. In the production of cooking chocolate, cocoa butter is replaced with other fats, sugars and oils to make it cheaper and sweeter. Although I love some confectionery chocolate (and hope you do too!) you should avoid it when making your own chocolates at home. What you need to buy is a chocolate that states what percentage of cocoa solids it has. For example, a 70% cocoa solids content is the industry standard for good chocolate.

70% isn't always best

You will often hear that 'you must use 70% chocolate for cooking' in recipe books, on television and by respected chefs, but this is not strictly true. As we have learnt already, cocoa beans from different areas of the world have very different flavours and thus intensity of flavour, and sometimes more than 70% and sometimes less than 70% cocoa content within a particular chocolate shows off that bean best. For example, chocolate from Ghana usually has quite a strong flavour so a lower cocoa content would be better when combining its flavour with others such as banana and hazelnuts so as not to overpower other delicate flavours within a dish.

For me, it's about matching the rest of the flavours in the dessert to the flavours naturally found in the chocolate. Some 60% chocolates have more robust flavours than 70% and chocolate with up to 95% cocoa content is readily available so it's about tasting and trying different chocolates before you transform them into delicious truffles, bakes and treats, so you know what you're working with.

Understanding chocolate

How long have we been enjoying chocolate?

Chocolate as we know it hasn't actually been around for very long. However, cocoa or cacao, from which chocolate derives, was first discovered by the Aztecs many centuries ago. Then, it was seen as the food of the gods so we really should treat it with the respect it deserves! Grown in the rainforests of the equatorial belt, it wasn't introduced to Europe until the 16th century when it was transported to Spain and was first consumed as a drink. It was not until much later, in the 19th century, that it was eaten in bar form.

Cocoa pods are grown on trees known as *theobroma cacao* which roughly translates from the Latin as 'food of the gods', or more literally 'God food'. To the Aztecs, cocoa was a source of spiritual wisdom, tremendous energy and enhanced sexual prowess. Known for their love of spices, they ground chilli and other spices with the cocoa beans and added hot water to make cocoa-based drinks. My Aztec hot chocolate (see page 150) and the other drinks in this book pay homage to this ancient technique for enjoying chocolate. In Aztec time, it was only consumed by high priests and people of authority and not by the common man. They drank it on a daily basis from golden cups and it was considered, as it is now, an exotic luxury; although it bore little resemblance to the smooth, rich and creamy chocolate we know today. The cocoa beans were so precious that they were often given as offerings to the gods alongside items such as precious stones, gold, silver and even jaguar skins!

Through modern research, we now know that chocolate offers many health benefits and contains natural sugars that do boost energy, going some way to explaining why the Aztecs gave it to their warriors to fortify them ahead of military campaigns. The Spanish soon caught onto this, and many food historians say that Hernán Cortés, a Spanish conquistador who led the expedition against the Aztecs, told Carlos I of Spain that the drink would help fight fatigue in their legions. And that it did as the Spanish overthrew the Aztecs and claimed much of Mexico for themselves towards the end of the 16th century.

It wasn't until the 19th century that a famous chocolatier named Rudolf Lindt, with the help of a Dutch chemist Daniel Peter, invented chocolate in bar form. Lindt developed the process known as 'conching' or melting the chocolate, while Peter's machine pressed the cocoa butter from the cocoa beans to form a liquor and combined it with dried milk, cream and sugar to alter the flavour and composition of cocoa. This helped the chocolate to become refined and smooth.

The bean to bar process of taking a cocoa pod/bean and turning it into the chocolate bars has evolved over centuries. But the chocolate we enjoy today was developed, and the process streamlined, by the introduction of the conching press in 1880. I take a brief look at the process of extracting cocoa and transforming it to chocolate on pages 18–19 which fascinates and excites chocolatiers and chocolate lovers.

In the 19th century these techniques were cutting edge, which made the cost to the consumer very high. Added to this, were the extremely high importation costs for both the cocoa and sugar, so chocolate remained the exclusive privilege of the rich and famous until the 20th century. Thankfully, since then, chocolate has gradually become more affordable.

Across Europe, the end of the 19th century and the beginning of the 20th century saw the establishment of the big names in the chocolate world who started producing chocolate for bakers, chocolatiers and pastry chefs. There was a boom in chocolate manufacturing that saw Belgian factories boom with employment. Among the first commercial manufacturers in the UK

were Fry's and the Cadbury brothers, both names you are certain to have heard of.

Today, chocolate is enjoyed around the globe and the chocolate industry is worth over £3 billion/ $5 billion. It is estimated that Britons alone eat on average just under 200 g/7 oz. of chocolate per person each week. That's a lot of chocolate! And all this growth is evidence of the truth we knew already: chocolate is delicious and people love to eat, drink, cook and bake with it. American artist and cartoonist John Q. Tullius summed it up best when he said, 'nine out of ten people like chocolate – the tenth person always lies.'

Where on earth does cocoa come from?

Chocolate is manufactured all over the world and most famously in Switzerland, France and Belgium. But chocolate is made from the processing of cocoa beans. The cocoa pods, containing the beans are cut from trees that are only grown in certain rainforests of the world found 20° north and 20° south of the Equator. According to many, South American cocoa is considered to be of the highest quality, but the largest producers are mainly in West Africa with many producers based in the Ivory Coast and Ghana.

Cocoa's origins can be traced back to the forests of Central American countries such as Mexico, Venezuela and Ecuador, and although these are not the largest producers, many artisan chocolate producers continue to select their cocoa beans from plantations in these three countries because of their heritage. Moreover, in recent years over 600,000 tonnes of cocoa has been cultivated in the Far East; in Malaysia, Vietnam, the Philippines and Papua New Guinea. Its production, although limited to the land mass within a 40° radius, is vast and widespread around the globe.

There are three main varieties of the cocoa tree – the Forastero, the Criollo and the Trinitario. Historically, Forastero and Criollo trees originated in Central and South America, and during the movement of cocoa in the early 1700s, the Criollo and Forastero were cross-pollinated to produce the Trinitaro plant.

The Forastero tree was transported to West Africa and has now become the most commonly cultivated in the world, and the one that Europeans have grown used to. Approximately 85% of the world's chocolate in production today originates from Forastero trees. Yet Trinitaro is also high yielding and robust, and is typically found in the Far East. Whereas the Criollo has a very small yield today but is still considered by many to be the source of the best flavoured bean.

The cocoa pod is much like the coffee cherry, in that it contains beans within its shell. Depending on where the cocoa is grown, each bean, as with coffee has a different taste. For example, just like in wine, the terroir, soil and landscape changes the way the wine or chocolate tastes, even if it's the same variety of grape or bean. Chocolate made with Criollo beans from the Dominican Republic characteristically tastes fruity and goes really well with red fruits such as raspberries. Whereas a chocolate made with Forestero beans from Ghana tastes of roasted nuts, so I always pair that type of chocolate with praline or bananas. No matter where your chocolate comes from there's a way to enhance its flavour with the recipes in this book. It's good to know too that these recipes can be made dairy- or gluten-free. When it comes to ganaches and truffles, use a high percentage dark/bittersweet chocolate and replace the cream with either water or fruit purées, and the butter with olive oil. When baking, use gluten-free flours mixed with a little bit of tapioca flour or a ratio of ground almonds or hazelnuts. And for desserts, simply replace any dairy cream and milk with nut or soy milk.

How chocolate is made: from bean to bar

Pod to bean

It is important to understand that a great chocolate taste starts with growing great cocoa beans. Manufacturers educate farmers about yield, disease resistance and soil management to grow healthy cocoa trees. Cocoa pods are harvested twice a year because they do not naturally fall from trees like apples – they must be cut down by machete. When the cocoa pod is harvested, it is cracked open and the beans, covered by a fleshy pulp that tastes like lychee, are scooped out and heaped up, covered with banana leaves and left to ferment for several days. Once fermented, the beans are dried, often left in the sun, again for several days. The dried beans will then be transported in bulk in hessian sacks loaded into cargo ships to the cocoa manufacturer where the process continues.

Bean to liquor

Once the beans arrive at the cocoa manufacturer, they go through several processes to discard any stones or other objects that could damage processing equipment. They can be blended or kept as a single origin bean. Some producers will mix beans from different regions, whereas others keep the bean pure to produce a particular type of chocolate. The beans are then roasted (and this is when the aromas and tastes of chocolate really become apparent) in their shells to preserve the delicate flavours. The time and temperature for roasting varies by manufacturer, as roasting affects flavour and each manufacturer has its distinct taste. A high temperature and long roast cycle will result in a high roasted flavour, and a shorter roast cycle will retain many of the bean's natural flavour.

 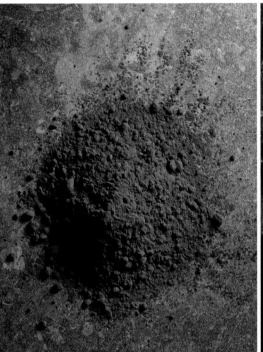 

Butter, liquor & powder

The roasted beans are then broken into cocoa nibs with a fat content greater than 50%, which can also be used in recipes for decoration or added bite. As the nibs are processed, the cocoa fat, known as cocoa butter is released, and as they continue to be ground are transformed into a liquid known as cocoa liquor. The cocoa liquor is then hydraulically pressed, drained and reserved, leaving pure cocoa powder from the bean. The cocoa liquor is used in the manufacture of chocolate through the addition of milk solids, sugar and flavourings. Depending upon each manufacturer's chocolate recipe, the cocoa liquor can be separated into its constituent parts; butter and powder, or used in liquor form. Typically, the cocoa butter is added into a conche with the other ingredients necessary to make chocolate.

Chocolate

The conching process introduces milk, sugar and flavourings to the cocoa butter and refines the chocolate through intense mixing for up to 72 hours. The chocolate mixture is constantly moved and the friction of the paddles used to stir it generates heat, which maintains a temperature of 60°C (140°F) and 75°C (165°F). Additional flavours such as vanilla can be added during the conching process to round off and balance the taste. Conching time and cocoa butter addition are crucial to the desired fluidity of the final chocolate. The chocolate, also known to chocolatiers and chefs as 'couverture' when it has a higher percentage of cocoa butter is now ready to use and will either be set into moulds or made into buttons, also known as 'callets'. It is then packed ready for us to buy, eat, work with and love!

Melting & Tempering

Melting

Melting is a really important process in the making of chocolates. If melting chocolate to temper with then it is often best to melt it in the microwave on a low heat, although you must take great care when doing so as it can easily burn and spoil. Some people melt chocolate in a *bain-marie* by setting a heatproof bowl over a saucepan or pot of simmering water. This is fine when you're making brownies and have butter in with the chocolate, but when melting chocolate for tempering, a *bain-marie* is not a good idea. If water splashes into the melting chocolate it will seize up, and it can also be affected by the steam. So, for me, always melt in the microwave.

Put the chocolate in a heatproof bowl and heat in the microwave in bursts of 30 seconds. Chocolate burns very easily so make sure you clean the sides of the bowl down after each burst of heat. **(A)**

Before tempering, make sure the chocolate is all melted and that you don't have any lumps left in. **(B)**

Tempering

You may have heard this term banded around by chefs and chocolatiers and not have a clue what it means. Without going into the science of re-crystallizing the crystals in the cocoa butter, it's basically the way the chocolate becomes shiny and glossy, and hardens with a crisp snap, not soft or bloomed. 'Blooming' is when the cocoa butter re-crystallizes on the surface of the chocolate often leaving a white residue. These steps are for tempering dark/bittersweet chocolate. For milk/semisweet or white, the technique is exactly the same but the temperatures are slightly different.

My preferred method of tempering is to use a marble slab, palette knife, scraper and an electric probe. It's important to say at this point to either use chocolate in button or callet form (see Resources page 174), or from a bar, chopped up finely – this will help melt the chocolate easier.

Tempering on the marble is the method I have used since I began working with chocolate and is my preferred method. However, there are other methods that are simpler and easy to master so try the one that appeals to you most.

E

F

The 'marble' technique

Melt the chocolate pieces, buttons (callets) to 45°C (110°F) for 30-second bursts in the microwave on a low heat. (**C, page 21**)

Pour out two thirds of the chocolate onto the clean, marble slab – it must be completely dry as any moisture on the marble will cause the chocolate to seize up. (**D, page 21**)

Begin to spread the chocolate thinly across the marble using a palette knife. This applies a shearing force to the chocolate, which along with temperature, is also critical to the tempering process. (**E**)

Bring the spread chocolate back together using a scraper, keep it moving and continue to shear and cool the chocolate. (**F**)

Continue to do so until the chocolate starts to thicken – you will see peaks form when the chocolate is dropped from the spatula. The cocoa butter within the chocolate is beginning to crystallize and the cooled mass should be 25°C (50°F). (**G**)

Working quickly, place the thickened, crystallized chocolate into the remaining chocolate in the bowl and stir thoroughly until the chocolate is smooth again, taking care to stir out any lumps. (**H**)

For dark/bittersweet chocolate, it should now be 32°C (90°F) and will be perfectly tempered. Milk/semisweet chocolate should be 29°C (85°F) and white should be 30°C (86°F).

To make sure the chocolate is well tempered (and it's always best to make sure), dip a little bit of torn baking parchment into the chocolate and place on your work surface to set a little. It should set hard within a few minutes at an ambient temperature.

The chocolate is now ready to use for moulding, dipping and decorating. Remember to work quickly and confidently with it to avoid further re-crystallization at room temperature.

The ʻseeding' technique (or adding more chocolate)

This is a good way to start your journey of mastering the art of tempering chocolate.

Weigh out the total amount of chocolate you need for the recipe, then remove one third of it and set aside. Melt the remaining two thirds of chocolate for 30-second bursts in the microwave on a low heat to 45°C (110°F). Then stir through the third you have reserved. Because the unmelted chocolate is already tempered, by adding it to the melted chocolate 45°C (110°F), you are stirring in the crystallized cocoa butter that you need to complete the tempering process.

Continue to stir until all the chocolate has melted. Check the temperature of the chocolate. For dark/bittersweet chocolate, it should now be 32°C (90°F) and will be perfectly tempered. Milk/semisweet chocolate should be 29°C (85°F) and white should be 30°C (86°F).

Tempering in the microwave

For small batches of chocolate, tempering in the microwave is best as it's so quick and doesn't make as much mess. Just like how we melted the chocolate for the marble technique, warm the chocolate for 30-second bursts in the microwave on a low heat, stirring between bursts.

It is important not to heat the chocolate too quickly as you want to crystallize the cocoa butter slowly, so reduce your microwave power to its lowest heat setting.

Once the chocolate is three quarters melted, stop heating. Stir the chocolate instead until all the remaining lumps have melted. Just like the marble method be sure to check the chocolate is tempered by dipping a little bit of torn baking parchment into the chocolate and place on your work surface to set a little. It should set within a few minutes.

The chocolate is now ready to use. Remember to work quickly and confidently with it.

Moulding

Chocolatiers have always used specially made moulds to create their wonderful concoctions. They used to be made from metal, but are now more commonly made from polycarbonate plastic. You can buy these polycarbonate moulds in lots of different shapes and sizes from various stores and websites, some of which are listed in Resources on page 174.

It's important that the moulds are totally clean and don't have any water near them, as any moisture will cause the chocolate to seize up. The easiest way to dry them after cleaning, is to blast them with a heat gun or hair dryer on a hot setting and wipe dry with a little cotton wool. Do not use paper towels or dish cloths as their fibres are too coarse and may scuff the moulds. Any small imperfection in the

mould will transfer to the chocolates and you will not achieve the clean, shiny effect you want from these moulds.

Once the chocolate has been tempered following the instructions on pages 20–23, spoon or pour the chocolate into your chosen mould. **(A)**

Working quickly, tip the mould to spread the chocolate, tapping the mould against the work surface to bash out any air bubbles that may be in the base of the mould. **(B)**

Hold the mould upside down and, using a scraper, tap the sides of the mould to knock any excess chocolate out. **(C)**

With the mould still upturned, scrape the surface of the mould to clean off the excess chocolate from around the sides, facing the table. **(D)**

Lay the mould face down on a baking sheet lined with greaseproof paper and set aside to firm up. Do not set the chocolate-lined mould in the fridge as this will shock the chocolate too much and may rush the crystallization process. (E, page 26)

Once the chocolate has set, you can then fill the moulds with your filling – in this case, a simple dark/bittersweet chocolate ganache (see pages 30–31). (F, page 26)

Allow the ganache to set at room temperature or in a cool, dark place then pour some remaining tempered chocolate over the top. (G, page 26)

Scrape any excess chocolate over the rest of the mould – this is known as 'capping off' – to seal the truffle. (H, page 26)

Set at room temperature until completely cold. Don't be tempted to chill in the fridge as this will alter the temperature too quickly and cause blooming.

Turn the mould upside down so that the bottoms of the chocolate face the work surface and tap the base of the mould down hard to release the chocolates. (I, page 27)

If you have cleaned the mould and tempered the chocolate correctly, the chocolates should contract once set making the truffles easy to pop out.

For best results, and if you don't want to get fingerprints on your nice shiny chocolates, wear cotton gloves when removing them from their moulds and transferring them onto a serving plate or into a gift box.

Dipping

Dipping chocolates, jellies and pralines is an age old tradition for chocolatiers. It's all about immersing the ganache or other filling into the tempered chocolate and taking off as much of the chocolate as you can. You don't want a thick outer case – the thinner you get it, the more professional your chocolates will look. I use a dipping fork, which you can buy online or from specialist kitchen suppliers, or you can simply use a normal kitchen fork. Make sure you have a baking sheet lined with baking parchment prepared to transfer your dipped chocolates.

Start by placing the bowl of tempered chocolate (see pages 20–23) onto a kitchen cloth and tip the bowl at an angle towards yourself – you don't want it overflowing, but it will help take some of the chocolate off later in the process. Dip the truffle into the tempered chocolate using a dipping fork, covering it completely. **(A)**

Dip a couple of times then pull the truffle out of the bowl quickly to remove some of the excess coating. **(B)**

Using the side of the bowl, bounce the truffle (on the fork) into the top of the chocolate. This will help pull down the chocolate from the top, leaving you with a thin coating all the way round the chocolate.

Pull the fork towards you against the bowl to take off the excess on the bottom of the truffle. **(C)**

Carefully tap the truffle onto the prepared baking sheet. If the truffle sticks to the fork, use a small sharp knife to lift it off. This takes a lot of practice so take your time.

To create the rippled effect on top of the truffles, place the fork into the top of the chocolate, pull up and drag the fork away. Again, this takes practice and I often dip once, then again to achieve a more pronounced ripple. **(D)**

D

Ganache

A ganache is most commonly referred to as a truffle filling. It is a rich, decadent set chocolate made with cream that can be used to make sauces and desserts, cover cakes and fill chocolates. The method is simple but the mixture can split or become temperamental, so it's about getting the quantities, temperatures and methods right. A ganache is an emulsification, such as mayonnaise where you want to emulsify fat and water, here, you want to make the cocoa butter and the fat in the cream come together to form a smooth ganache.

If the mixture does split, add a dash of cold milk and this should bring it back together. Don't boil the cream too much as this will cause trouble. You can substitute the dairy with nut and soy milks, or with fruit pureés or even water.

Single quantity

200 ml/1 cup whipping/heavy cream

a pinch of salt

200 g/1½ cups chopped milk/semisweet chocolate

200 g/1½ cups chopped dark/bittersweet chocolate

30 g/2 tablespoons unsalted butter

Makes about 600 g/21 oz.

Double quantity

400 ml/2 cups whipping/heavy cream

a pinch of salt

400 g/3 cups chopped milk/semisweet chocolate

400 g/3 cups chopped dark/bittersweet chocolate

60 g/4 tablespoons unsalted butter

Makes about 1.2 kg/42 oz.

Put the cream in a saucepan or pot set over a low–medium heat and slowly bring to the boil. Immediately remove from the heat and set aside to cool for a few minutes.

Pour the cream over the chocolate and set aside for 30 seconds to allow the chocolate to melt in the heat of the hot cream. **(A, B)**

Gently mix the ingredients using a handheld electric mixer or a spatula in a tight circular motion in the centre of the bowl, until the chocolate starts to melt and emulsify with the cream. Gradually widen the circle until all the chocolate has melted and you have a shiny, smooth ganache. **(C)**

Once emulsified, stir with a spatula to make sure there are no lumps and all the cream and chocolate have been incorporated. **(D)** You'll then be left with a shiny, rich, velvety truffle ganache.

Set aside to cool at room temperature for 3–4 hours before using. If still warm, the ganache may melt the tempered chocolate cases or truffle spheres.

You can add flavourings such as hazelnut purée and vanilla to this basic ganache recipe to better suit the flavours of your chosen chocolates, bakes or desserts. Some recipes within this book call for a slightly tweaked ganache.

Chocolates & truffles

Classic truffles

White or milk/semisweet
chocolate truffles
**100 ml/⅓ cup whipping/
heavy cream**
**25 g/2 tablespoons
unsalted butter**
a pinch of salt
**450 g/3¼ cups white
or milk/semisweet
chocolate, chopped**
**50 white or milk/
semisweet chocolate
truffle spheres**

*Dark/bittersweet chocolate
truffles (see page 37)*

*a disposable piping/pastry
bag*

Makes about 50

When you buy good chocolate, there is sometimes nothing better than a simple ganache to show off its quality and flavour. These simple, hand-rolled truffles are the first port of call for any budding chocolatier and make wonderful gifts for friends and family. The store-bought chocolate truffle spheres (a type of mould) also help you achieve a professional finish.

To make white or milk/semisweet chocolate truffles, follow this method. For dark/bittersweet chocolate truffles see page 37.

Put the cream, butter and salt into a small saucepan or pot set over a low heat and bring to the boil.

Tip 250 g/2 cups chopped chocolate into a bowl and pour over the hot cream mixture. Gently mix the ingredients using a spatula in a tight circular motion in the centre of the bowl, until the chocolate starts to melt and emulsify with the cream. Gradually widen the circle until all the chocolate has melted and you have a shiny, smooth ganache. Set aside to cool at room temperature for 3–4 hours.

Remove the protective lid on the chocolate spheres and leave in their plastic holder ready to fill. **(A)**

Scoop the cooled ganache into a disposable piping/pastry bag. Snip the end to create a nozzle/tip, pipe ganache into each sphere and let set in a cool, dark place. **(B, C)**

Temper the remaining chocolate according to the instructions on pages 20–23.

Roll each filled truffle sphere in tempered chocolate to coat completely. Then roll in your hand to alter the temperature of the chocolate and to achieve a textured finish. **(D, page 36)** Transfer to a sheet of baking parchment to set firm before serving. **(E, page 37)**

Dark/bittersweet chocolate truffles

**175 ml/¾ cup whipping/
heavy cream**

**15 g/1 tablespoon
unsalted butter**

**50 g/¼ cup golden caster/
granulated sugar**

a pinch of salt

**425 g/3 cups dark/
bittersweet chocolate,
chopped**

**50 dark/bittersweet
chocolate truffle
spheres**

*a disposable piping/pastry
bag*

Makes about 50

For dark/bittersweet chocolate truffles, put the cream, butter, sugar and salt into a small saucepan or pot set over a low heat and bring to the boil. Stir to melt the butter and dissolve the sugar.

Tip 225 g/1⅔ cups chopped chocolate into a bowl and pour over the hot cream mixture. Gently mix the ingredients using a spatula in a tight circular motion in the centre of the bowl, until the chocolate starts to melt and emulsify with the cream. Gradually widen the circle until all the chocolate has melted and you have a shiny, smooth ganache. Set aside to cool at room temperature for 3–4 hours.

Remove the protective lid on the chocolate spheres and leave in their plastic holder ready to fill. **(A, page 35)**

Scoop the cooled ganache into a disposable piping/pastry bag. Snip the end to create a nozzle/tip, pipe ganache into each sphere and let set in a cool, dark place. **(B, C, page 35)**

Temper the remaining chocolate according to the instructions on pages 20–23.

Roll each filled truffle sphere in tempered chocolate to coat completely. Then roll in your hand to alter the temperature of the chocolate and to achieve a textured finish. **(D)** Transfer to a sheet of baking parchment to set firm before serving. **(E)**

Variation
You can mix and match the types of chocolate ganache, spheres and coating to make a variety of classic truffles in the same way.

Classic champagne truffles

This is one of the most iconic chocolate truffles around. Sold all over the world and nearly always dusted with icing/confectioners' sugar, they are often made with a champagne-flavoured compound known as 'Marc de Champagne', but mine are made with the real thing! Yes, it's extravagant, but why not? You can of course use more or less Champagne, reduce the quantity of cream or even try using pink fizz. The addition of brandy just helps the flavours along.

40–50 dark/bittersweet chocolate truffle spheres

250 g/2 cups dark/ bittersweet chocolate, to temper

100 g/¾ cup icing/ confectioners' sugar

3 teaspoons cornflour/ cornstarch

Ganache

100 ml/⅓ cup double/ heavy cream

a pinch of salt

150 g/1¼ cups milk/ semisweet chocolate, chopped

100 g/¾ cup dark/ bittersweet chocolate, chopped

65 ml/¼ cups Champagne

2 teaspoons brandy or Cognac

a disposable piping/pastry bag

2 baking sheets, 1 lined with baking parchment

Makes 40–50

Begin by preparing the ganache. Put the cream and salt into a small saucepan or pot set over a low heat and bring to the boil.

Tip the chopped chocolates into a bowl and pour over the hot cream mixture. Stir briefly, then set aside for 3 minutes to allow the chocolate to melt in the heat of the hot cream. Add the Champagne and brandy and stir until all the chocolate has melted and you have a shiny, smooth ganache. Set aside to cool at room temperature for 3–4 hours.

Remove the protective lid on the chocolate spheres and leave in their plastic holder ready to fill.

Scoop the cooled ganache into a disposable piping/pastry bag. Snip the end to create

a nozzle/tip, pipe ganache into each sphere and let set in a cool, dark place.

Temper the dark/bittersweet chocolate according to the instructions on pages 20–23.

Sift the icing/confectioners' sugar and cornflour/cornstarch together onto the unlined baking sheet.

To finish, dip each of the filled truffles in the tempered chocolate to coat. Remove them using a dipping fork, tapping the fork on the side of the bowl to allow any excess chocolate to drip back into the bowl. Drop each truffle into the sugar mixture and roll to coat. Repeat with the remaining truffles, then transfer the coated truffles to the lined baking sheet to set firm before serving.

Whiskey & ginger barrels

On a recent visit to Ireland, I had the opportunity to visit the home of my favourite whiskey; Jameson. There I learnt how the whiskey is matured in three different casks and used for other spirits; sherry butts, bourbon barrels and port pipes. Whiskey and dry ginger is a drink my parents used to enjoy with my grandparents, so I hope they like my interpretation. A little squeeze of lime in the stem ginger works really well too!

175 ml/¾ cup whipping/ heavy cream
40 g/⅓ cup fresh ginger, peeled and finely chopped
15 g/1 tablespoon unsalted butter
40 g/3 tablespoons light muscovado sugar
a pinch of salt
60 ml/4 tablespoons whiskey (I use Jameson)
225 g/1⅔ cups dark/ bittersweet chocolate, chopped
300 g/2½ cups milk/ semisweet chocolate
50 g/⅓ cup stem ginger, finely chopped
freshly squeezed juice of 1 lime

28 log-shaped moulds, brushed with bronze lustre
2 disposable piping/pastry bags

Makes 28

Pour the cream into a small saucepan or pot set over a low heat. Add the chopped fresh ginger and bring to the boil. Remove from the heat and set aside for at least 30 minutes to allow the flavours to infuse.

Return the cream to the heat, add the butter, sugar and salt, and bring to a gentle boil, stirring to melt the butter and dissolve the sugar. Add 45 ml/3 tablespoons of whiskey and stir again.

Tip the dark/bittersweet chocolate into a bowl and pour over the hot cream. Gently mix the ingredients using a spatula in a tight circular motion in the centre of the bowl, until the chocolate starts to melt and emulsify with the cream. Gradually widen the circle until all the chocolate has melted and you have a shiny, smooth ganache. Set aside to cool at room temperature for 3–4 hours.

Temper the milk/semisweet chocolate according to the instructions on pages 20–23.

Coat the log shaped moulds with tempered chocolate according to the instructions on pages 24–27 and let set at room temperature.

Meanwhile, put the stem ginger in a food processor with the lime juice and remaining whiskey. Blitz until smooth and spoon into a disposable piping/pastry bag. Snip the end to create a nozzle/tip, pipe the stem ginger purée into each moulded shell and set aside.

Scoop the cooled ganache into a disposable piping/pastry bag. Snip the end to create a nozzle/tip, pipe ganache on top of the stem ginger purée into each moulded shell and set in a cool, dark place.

Once the ganache has set, cover the tops of the barrels with more tempered chocolate to seal according to the instructions on pages 24–27 and let set before popping out of the moulds to serve.

Amaretto & toasted marzipan truffles

When my sister and I were children, our Nans regularly made one of three different cakes, the Chocolate fudge cake (page 93) being one and another being a fruit and nut cake topped marzipan and white icing. We hated the marzipan then, but I've grown to love it, especially when it's toasted. Topped with a luscious amaretto ganache, it really is a lovely combination of all things sweet and almond!

150 g/½ cup natural-coloured marzipan
30 g/⅓ cup amaretti cookies, finely crushed
1 tablespoon seedless apricot jam/jelly
225 g/1⅔ cups dark/bittersweet chocolate, finely chopped
75 g/½ cup milk/semisweet chocolate, finely chopped
125 ml/½ cup whipping/heavy cream
40 g/3 tablespoons light muscovado sugar
3 tablespoons Amaretto di Saronno or other almond liqueur
a pinch of salt
250 g/2 cups dark/bittersweet chocolate, to temper

an 18-cm/7-inch square pan, lined with baking parchment

Makes about 40

Preheat the oven to 170°C (325°F) Gas 3.

Roll out the marzipan onto a lightly sugared surface into an 18-cm/7-inch square – use the base of the baking pan as a guide. Scatter with half of the crushed amaretti and press the crumbs into the marzipan using a rolling pin, dusted with icing/confectioners' sugar. Flip the marzipan over so that the amaretti are on the underside and press the marzipan evenly and neatly into the base of the prepared baking pan. Bake on the middle shelf of the preheated oven for 5–6 minutes.

Meanwhile, heat the apricot jam/jelly in a small saucepan or pot set over a low heat until runny. Strain with a fine mesh sieve or strainer into a bowl to remove any lumps and set aside.

Remove the marzipan from the oven and set aside to cool for a few minutes, then brush the top with the warmed and strained jam/jelly.

To make the ganache, pour the cream into a small saucepan or pot set over a low–medium heat. Add the sugar, amaretto and salt, and bring to the boil, stirring all the time to dissolve the sugar. Tip the chopped chocolates into a bowl and pour over the hot cream mixture. Set aside for 30 seconds to allow the chocolate to melt in the heat of the hot cream, then stir until smooth.

Pour the ganache over the jam/jelly-topped marzipan and spread level using an off-set palette knife. Set in a cool, dark place until cold, cover and set aside at room temperature for 3–4 hours, until firm.

Once set, carefully lift the layered marzipan from the pan, trim the edges and, using a warmed knife, cut the ganache into 1½-cm/½-inch square truffles.

Temper the remaining dark/bittersweet chocolate according to the instructions on pages 20–23.

Dip each of the truffles in the tempered chocolate to coat. Remove them using a dipping fork, tapping the fork on the side of the bowl to allow any excess chocolate to drip back into the bowl (see page 28). Repeat with the remaining truffles, then place the coated truffles on a clean sheet of baking parchment.

To finish, scatter the remaining crushed amaretti to one side on top of each truffle.

A   B   C

Earl Grey & orange marmalade truffles

Tea and marmalade has to be one of my favourite flavour combinations. It's like eating and drinking breakfast at the same time; marmalade on toast washed down with a cup of fragrant tea, or the most extravagant Jaffa Cake you'll ever eat!

Orange pâte de fruit
3 oranges
175 g/¾ cups caster/
granulated sugar
45 ml/3 tablespoons
apple-based liquid
pectin
1 teaspoon freshly
squeezed lemon juice

Ganache
2 tablespoons loose-leaf
Earl Grey tea
25 g/2 tablespoons soft
brown sugar
a few drops of food-grade
bergamot oil, optional
175 g/1⅓ cups milk/
semisweet chocolate,
finely chopped
200 g/1½ cups dark/
bittersweet chocolate
(70%), finely chopped

continued overleaf

To make the *pâte de fruit*, place one orange in a small saucepan or pot set over a medium heat, cover with cold water and bring to the boil. Reduce the heat to a gentle simmer and continue to cook for 10 minutes to soften the skin of the orange. Drain and discard the water and let the orange cool for 2–3 minutes.

Cut a thin slice from the top and bottom of the cooked orange and discard. Then cut the orange into quarters and remove any seeds as well as the central, pithy core. Cut the quarters into rough chunks and whizz in the food processor until almost smooth. Push the orange pulp through a fine mesh sieve or strainer and weigh the resulting purée – you will need 100 g–125 g/⅓–½ cup. Squeeze the juice from the remaining oranges – you will need 200 ml/¾ cup.

Tip 75 g/⅓ cup of the sugar into a small heavy-bottomed saucepan or pot set over a low–medium heat. Add 1 tablespoon of water and dissolve the sugar without stirring. Bring to the boil and continue to cook until the sugar becomes an amber-coloured caramel. Swirl the pan if necessary to ensure the caramel cooks evenly. Remove the pan from the heat and carefully add the orange juice, strained orange purée and remaining 100 g/ ½ cup of sugar. Stir until smooth and return to a low heat to dissolve any hardened caramel. Bring to a steady, gentle simmer and cook the mixture until it reaches 107°C (220°F). **(A)**

Add the pectin and lemon juice, stir to combine and simmer gently until the mixture reaches 107°C (220°F) again. Simmer at this temperature for 2 minutes, stirring frequently.

E

F

To finish
**250 g/2 cups milk/
  semisweet chocolate,
  to temper**
bronze lustre powder
**2 tablespoons clear
  alcohol such as vodka
  or gin**

*an 18-cm/7-inch square pan,
  lined with clingfilm/plastic
  wrap*
*a small, fluted, round cookie
  cutter, warmed in hot water*
*a sponge-headed brush
  (available from art shops
  or online)*

Makes 20–30

Spoon ½ teaspoon of the mixture onto a cold plate and leave for 30 seconds. If the *pâte de fruit* is ready it should wrinkle when pushed with the tip of your finger. **(B, page 45)**

Remove the pan from the heat, leave for 1 minute for the bubbling to subside, then pour the orange mixture into the prepared pan. Set aside for at least 2 hours, until firm.

Meanwhile prepare the ganache. Tip the loose-leaf tea into a saucepan or pot set over a low heat. Add 200 ml/¾ cup water and bring slowly to the boil. Remove from the heat and set aside for at least 2 hours to allow the flavours to infuse.

Add the sugar to the tea infusion and bring slowly back to the boil. Strain through a fine mesh sieve or strainer into a jug/pitcher – you will need 150 ml/⅔ cup.

Tip both the chopped chocolates into a bowl and pour over the hot tea. Set aside for 30 seconds to allow the chocolate to melt in the heat of the hot tea, then stir until smooth.

Pour the ganache over the set *pâte de fruit*, spread level using an off-set palette knife. Chill in the fridge for 30 minutes, until firm.

Once set, lift the ganache out of the pan and using the warm cookie cutter, cut out discs of the layered truffle and place on a clean sheet of baking parchment. **(C, page 45)**

To finish, temper the remaining milk/semisweet chocolate according to the instructions on pages 20–23.

Follow the instructions for dipping the truffles on pages 28–29, coat each truffle in tempered chocolate and arrange on a clean sheet of baking parchment. **(D)**

For a final flourish, mix some bronze lustre powder with a little bit of clear alcohol to make a liquid paste – not too thick but not too runny. **(E)** Then, using a sponge brush, stamp the bronze paste across the one side of the tops of each set truffle. **(F)** The alcohol will evaporate when it dries leaving the lovely metallic pattern.

Chocolates & truffles 47

Hazelnut truffles

This famous round, chocolate and hazelnut truffle is loved across the world. My version includes a crunchy feuilletine base, which is made of a baked and crushed French wafer that you can buy online, mixed with hazelnut praline paste and chocolate, topped with a hazelnut ganache and a whole roasted hazelnut. You can also turn this into a fantastic dessert by making one big truffle in a large cake pan, topped with lots of hazelnuts and drizzled with melted chocolate.

Feuilletine base
90 g/⅔ cup milk/ semisweet chocolate, chopped
25 g/1½ tablespoons unsalted butter
50 g/¼ cup hazelnut paste
90 g/1 cup feuilletine

Hazelnut ganache
150 ml/⅔ cups whipping/ heavy cream
335 g/2¾ cups milk/ semisweet chocolate, finely chopped
40 g/3 tablespoons clear honey
90 g/scant ½ cup hazelnut paste

To finish
250 g/2 cups dark/ bittersweet chocolate
50 g/½ cups hazelnuts, toasted
75 g/½ cup milk/ semisweet chocolate

a 26 x 18-cm/10 x 7-inch baking pan, greased and lined with baking parchment
a 3-cm/1¼-inch round cookie cutter, warmed in hot water
a disposable piping/pastry bag

Makes about 35 truffles

Start by making the crunchy feuilletine base. Melt the chocolate and butter in a heatproof bowl set over a saucepan or pot of barely simmering water. Stir until smooth and let cool slightly. Add the hazelnut paste and feuilletine and mix until thoroughly combined. Scoop the mixture into the prepared baking pan and, using the back of a spoon, press into a thin, even layer covering the base. Chill in the fridge until firm while you prepare the ganache.

Tip all of the ganache ingredients into a heatproof bowl set over a saucepan or pot of barely simmering water. Stir gently to combine until you have a silky smooth mixture. Remove from the heat and cool slightly before pouring over the crisp, chilled feuilletine base. Spread level using an off-set palette knife and set in a cool, dark place until cold. Cover and set aside at room temperature for 3–4 hours, or overnight, until firm.

Temper the dark/bittersweet chocolate according to the instructions on pages 20–23.

Once set, lift the ganache out of the pan and using the warm cookie cutter, cut out discs of the layered truffle and place on a clean sheet of baking parchment – cut the circles as close together as possible to avoid too much wastage and to ensure that you get the maximum amount of truffles from the mixture.

Lightly press a toasted hazelnut into the top of each truffle.

Follow the instructions for dipping the truffles on pages 28–29, coat each truffle in tempered chocolate and arrange on a clean sheet of baking parchment. (D)

Temper the milk/semisweet chocolate according to the instructions on pages 20–23. Spoon the tempered chocolate into a disposable piping/pastry bag, snip the end into a fine point and drizzle the milk chocolate over the truffles to decorate.

Rum & raisin chocolate fudge

This is one of my Dad's favourites. As a family we have always gone to the Isle of Wight for summer holidays and if rum and raisin flavoured ice cream is ever on the menu or being scooped at Strollers Café, my Dad always orders it. Chocolate and rum go really well together, and the juicy rum-soaked raisins work perfectly in this simple yet spectacular fudge!

100 g/²⁄₃ cup (dark) raisins

50 ml/¼ cup dark or spiced rum

½ vanilla pod/bean, split

500 g/2½ cups caster/granulated sugar

170 g/¾ cups evaporated milk

170 ml/¾ cup whole milk

50 g/3½ tablespoons unsalted butter

a pinch of salt

125 g/1 cup dark/bittersweet chocolate (70%), chopped

1 tablespoon cocoa powder, sifted

an 18–20-cm/7–8-inch square pan, lined with baking parchment

Makes about 40 pieces

Tip the raisins, rum and the split vanilla pod/bean into a small saucepan or pot set over a low heat. Gently warm the rum but do not allow it to boil. Stir well, remove the pan from the heat and set aside until the mixture is cold and the raisins are plump, juicy and have absorbed all of the vanilla-scented rum.

Put the sugar into a large, heavy-bottomed saucepan or pot with a capacity of at least 2½ litres/11 cups. Add the evaporated milk, whole milk, butter and salt. Simmer over a medium heat and stir gently to dissolve the sugar. Put a sugar thermometer into the pan and bring the mixture to the boil, reduce the heat and continue to cook, without stirring, at a low, steady boil until the mixture reaches 114°C (230°F). Add the remaining rum and immediately remove the pan from the heat.

Set aside for a few minutes until the bubbling subsides.

Tip the chopped chocolate and sifted cocoa powder into a large mixing bowl and pour over the hot fudge mixture. Stir gently to combine and set aside to cool for 10 minutes.

Using a wooden spoon or rubber spatula, beat the fudge until it thickens, cools and becomes slightly grainy. Add the rum soaked raisins and mix to thoroughly combine. Pour the fudge into the prepared baking pan and spread level using the back of a spoon or a palette knife. Set in a cool, dark place for 3–4 hours, or overnight, until firm.

Once firm, cut the fudge into small squares before serving or store in an airtight container for up to 1 week – if it lasts that long!

Thyme & honey truffles

When I won the first Medallion of Excellence for a British pastry chef at the international WorldSkills competition in Japan in 2007, this formed part of my chocolate collection. The distinct taste of herbs in chocolates and desserts has become really trendy in the last few years and this combination works really well as thyme and honey are both quite delicate. Also rosemary, lemon and even basil work very well with chocolate.

250 g/2 cups tempered dark/bittersweet chocolate

Ganache
150 ml/²⁄₃ cup double/ heavy cream
2 teaspoons fresh thyme leaves, plus 40 to garnish
50 g/3½ tablespoons clear honey
a pinch of salt
200 g/1½ cups dark/ bittersweet chocolate (66%), chopped
40 g/3 tablespoons unsalted butter, at room temperature and diced

To finish
clear honey
caster/granulated sugar

a disposable piping/pastry bag
40 square truffle moulds

Makes 40

Begin by preparing the ganache. Put the cream, thyme leaves, honey and salt into a small saucepan or pot set over a low heat and bring slowly to the boil. Remove from the heat and set aside for at least 1 hour to allow the flavours to infuse.

Meanwhile, prepare the truffle cases. Temper the dark/bittersweet chocolate according to the instructions on pages 20–23.

Coat the square truffle moulds with tempered chocolate according to the instructions on pages 24–27 and let set at room temperature.

Tip the chopped chocolate into a bowl and add the diced butter. Bring the infused cream slowly back to the boil and then pass through a fine mesh sieve or strainer over the chopped chocolate. Set aside for a minute to allow the chocolate to melt in the heat of the hot cream, then stir until silky smooth. Set aside until cold but still runny enough to pipe.

Scoop the cooled ganache into a disposable piping/pastry bag. Snip the end to create a nozzle/tip, pipe ganache into each moulded case, leaving a gap of 1–2 mm/¹⁄₁₆–¹⁄₈ inch at the top. Set in a cool, dark place until firm.

Once the ganache has set, cover the tops of the truffles with more tempered chocolate to seal according to the instructions on pages 24–27 and set firm before popping out of the moulds.

Preheat the oven to 170°C (325°F) Gas 3.

To make the crystallized thyme leaves, dip the thyme leaves in honey and place on the prepared baking sheet. Bake in the preheated oven for about 5 minutes, until the leaves become crisp. Remove from the oven and scatter sugar over the still-warm leaves.

The mould I use leaves a glossy finish across one corner of each truffle.

Pipe a small dot of tempered chocolate onto the shiny corner of the moulded chocolates and carefully place a crystallized thyme leaf on each truffle and serve.

Lemon & white chocolate drops

One of my career highlights was when, still at the University of West London, I won the Royal Academy of Culinary Arts Annual Awards of Excellence in Pastry, and this chocolate, although made with passion fruit at the time, was one of the chocolates that helped me win. Coincidently it wasn't the first time this particular chocolate led to an award, in 2000 it helped me to achieve the coveted Master of Culinary Arts (MCA) status for my mentor, friend and top pastry chef Yolande Stanley. It takes a lot of practice to perfect the right texture to pipe the ganache but once mastered it is a joy to behold, as well as delicious!

freshly squeezed juice of 2 lemons and the grated zest of ½
100 g/½ cup caster/granulated sugar
3 egg yolks
75 g/⅓ cup double/heavy cream
330 g/3¾ cups white chocolate, chopped
50 g/3½ tablespoons unsalted butter, diced and softened
2–3 drops lemon oil (optional)
250 g/2 cups dark/bittersweet chocolate, tempered
gold leaf, to finish

a large piping/pastry bag fitted with a plain nozzle/tip
a baking sheet, lined with baking parchment

Makes about 40

Put the lemon juice into a small saucepan or pot set over a medium heat and bring to the boil. Continue to boil until you have just 30 g/1 tablespoon remaining.

Whisk the sugar with the egg yolks for 2 minutes, until pale and creamy. Add the cream, reduced lemon juice and lemon zest, and whisk again until combined.

Scoop the mixture into a small heavy-bottomed pan and set over a low heat. Stirring all the time, cook for about 3 minutes, until the mixture thickens. Do not be tempted to turn up the heat – it will thicken in time and you risk scorching or scrambling the delicate mixture.

Tip the chopped white chocolate into a bowl with the butter and set aside.

Pass the lemon mixture through a fine mesh sieve or strainer over the white chocolate. Set aside for 30 seconds to allow the chocolate to melt in the heat of the hot lemon mixture, then stir until smooth. Add the lemon oil, if using, stir again and set aside at room temperature until cold and firm. Chill in the fridge for 15 minutes.

Spoon the ganache into the prepared piping/pastry bag and pipe 40 even sized mounds onto the prepared baking sheet. Chill in the fridge until firm.

Temper the dark/bittersweet chocolate according to the instructions on pages 20–23.

Dip each of the truffles in the tempered chocolate to coat. Remove them using a dipping fork, tapping the fork on the side of the bowl to allow any excess chocolate to drip back into the bowl. Repeat with the remaining truffles, then place the coated truffles on a clean sheet of baking parchment.

To finish, using a small, sharp knife, place a small amount of gold leaf on the point of each truffle.

Strawberry & balsamic vinegar truffles

The Italians have been macerating strawberries in balsamic vinegar for years now. I like to think of this as a 'harmonious contradiction' in that it shouldn't really work, but it definitely does! The freeze-dried strawberry pieces, which you can now buy from various supermarkets and online, add an extra burst of strawberry flavour when you bite through the crisp white chocolate shell.

200 g/2 cups strawberries, hulled and quartered
1 tablespoon freshly squeezed lemon juice
1 tablespoon icing/confectioners' sugar
50 ml/¼ cup whipping/heavy cream
a pinch of salt
300 g/2½ cups white chocolate, chopped
2–3 teaspoons aged balsamic vinegar
red food colouring paste
50 white chocolate truffle spheres

To finish
200 g/1½ cups white chocolate
6 g/¼ oz. freeze-dried strawberry pieces

a disposable piping/pastry bag

Makes 50

Whizz the strawberries in a food processor with the lemon juice and icing/confectioners' sugar, until smooth. Pass the purée through a fine mesh sieve or strainer into a small saucepan or pot set over a low–medium heat. Cook the purée, stirring all the time, until it has reduced by half and weighs 100 g/⅓ cup. Add the cream and salt, stir to combine and simmer for 1 minute.

Tip 300 g/2½ cups chopped chocolate into a bowl and pour over the hot cream mixture. Gently mix the ingredients together using a spatula in a tight circular motion in the centre of the bowl, until the chocolate starts to melt and emulsify with the cream. Gradually widen the circle until all the chocolate has melted and you have a shiny, smooth ganache.

Gradually add the balsamic vinegar. Taste the ganache after you have added 2 teaspoons and decide if you need to add more. Add a tiny amount of red food colouring paste, just enough to enhance the strawberry red colour, and stir until thoroughly combined. Set aside to cool at room temperature for 3–4 hours.

Scoop the cooled ganache into a disposable piping/pastry bag. Snip the end to create a nozzle/tip, pipe ganache into each sphere and let set in a cool, dark place.

Temper the remaining white chocolate according to the instructions on pages 20–23. Add the freeze-dried strawberry pieces and mix well.

Roll each filled truffle sphere in tempered chocolate to coat completely. Then roll in your hand to alter the temperature of the chocolate and to achieve a textured finish. Transfer to a sheet of baking parchment to set firm before serving.

Raspberry, redcurrant & rose truffles

This fragrant and very fruity chocolate really packs a powerful punch – just how I like my chocolates! We all know that raspberries and chocolate are a match made in heaven but adding the astringent tanginess of redcurrant and the floral beauty of rose, takes the combination to a whole new level in this simple ganache encased in a tempered chocolate shell.

100 g/⅔ cup raspberries

100 g/1 cup redcurrants, de-stalked

2 teaspoons freshly squeezed lemon juice

1 tablespoon caster/ granulated sugar

100 g/¾ cup dark/ bittersweet chocolate (at least 65%), chopped

100 ml/⅓ cup milk/ semisweet chocolate, chopped

a few drops of rosewater, rose extract or food-grade rose oil

To finish

250 g/2 cups dark/ bittersweet chocolate

freeze-dried rose petals, to decorate

a disposable piping/pastry bag

40 oval moulds

Makes 40

Begin by preparing the ganache. Put the raspberries and redcurrants into a small saucepan or pot set over a low–medium heat. Add the lemon juice and sugar and cook the fruit for 2–3 minutes, stirring often, until it has softened, burst and become juicy.

Pass the contents of the pan through a fine mesh sieve or strainer into a clean saucepan or pot. Add 45 ml/3 tablespoons of water and bring slowly to the boil.

Tip the chopped chocolates into a bowl and pour over the hot fruit mixture. Set aside for 2 minutes to allow the chocolate to melt in the heat of the hot fruit mixture. Add the rosewater, then stir until smooth. Set aside at room temperature until cold but not set completely.

Meanwhile, prepare the truffle cases. Temper the dark/bittersweet chocolate according to the instructions on pages 20–23.

Coat the oval truffle moulds with tempered chocolate according to the instructions on pages 24–27 and let set at room temperature.

Scoop the cooled ganache into a disposable piping/pastry bag. Snip the end to create a nozzle/tip, pipe ganache into each case, leaving a gap of 1–2 mm/1/16–1/8 inch at the top. Set in a cool, dark place until firm.

Once the ganache has set, cover the tops of the truffles with more tempered chocolate to seal according to the instructions on pages 24–27. Pipe a small amount of tempered chocolate onto one end of the truffles, decorating each chocolate with a freeze-dried rose petal.

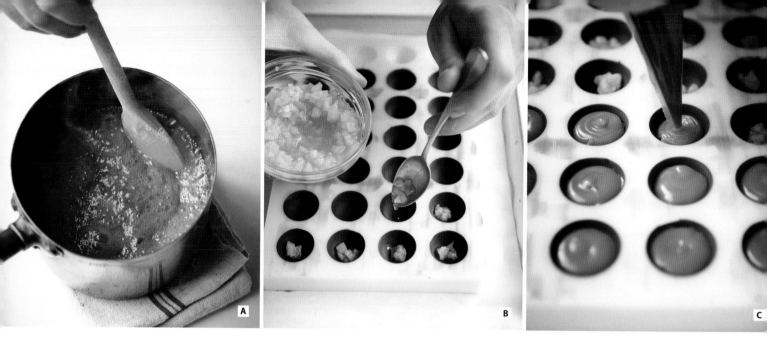

A   B   C

Cognac, caramel & pear domes

100 g/1 cup canned pear, drained and finely diced

50 ml/¼ cup Cognac

250 g/2 cups caster/granulated sugar

100 ml/⅓ cup whipping/heavy cream

1 star anise

25 g/1½ tablespoons unsalted butter

a pinch of salt

28 dark/bittersweet chocolate truffle domes

50 g/⅓ cup dark/bittersweet chocolate, melted

200 g/1½ cups dark/bittersweet chocolate, tempered (page 20–23)

gold lustre (optional)

28 half-dome moulds
a disposable piping/pastry bag

Makes 28

As part of a UK delegation to the International Cognac Summit, I was tasked with matching food with different types of Cognac. The subtle biscuity cookie flavour and light caramel viscosity, is perfect to make a caramel with and for pairing with pears drowned in cognac, as I've done here!

Tip the finely diced pear into a small bowl with 2 teaspoons of Cognac and leave to marinade for at least 2 hours.

To make the caramel, tip the sugar into a large, heavy-bottomed saucepan or pot with a capacity of at least 2½ litres/11 cups – the caramel will bubble furiously in the pan later so you will need a slightly larger pan. Add 1 tablespoon of water and dissolve the sugar without stirring. Bring to the boil and continue to cook until the sugar becomes an amber-coloured caramel. Swirl the pan if necessary to ensure the caramel cooks evenly. **(A)**

As the caramel is cooking and in a separate saucepan or pot set over a low heat, just boil the cream with the star anise.

Working quickly, gradually strain the hot cream into the pan with the caramel – take

care as it will splutter – and stir with a long handled wooden spoon or spatula until smooth. Add the remaining Cognac, butter and salt, and stir again until smooth. Return the pan to a low heat, simmer for 30 seconds and pour into a clean bowl to cool.

Spoon a little of the Cognac-soaked pear into each truffle dome. **(B)** Scoop the caramel into a disposable piping/pastry bag. Snip the end to create a nozzle/tip, pipe caramel into each dome. **(C)** Spoon the melted dark/bittersweet chocolate into another bag and pipe into the opening of each truffle shell to seal the caramel inside. Set in a cool, dark place until firm.

Once the ganache has set, cover the tops of the domes with more tempered chocolate to seal according to the instructions on pages 24–27. Brush with gold lustre and serve.

Salted brown sugar caramel truffles

I love dark brown sugar, especially muscovado. When boiled with cream and poured over a sticky toffee pudding, it is my idea of food heaven. And mixed with dark and smoky chocolate it gives you a completely different taste experience. Here instead of a traditional salted caramel recipe, I blend the flavour of deep, rich and treacly muscovado with cream and make it into a ganache with dark chocolate – a little bit different, but a new experience for all you legions of salted caramel lovers out there!

Ganache
100 g/½ cup dark muscovado sugar
25 g/1½ tablespoons unsalted butter
250 ml/1 cup whipping/ heavy cream
seeds from ½ vanilla pod/ bean or 1 teaspoon pure vanilla extract
250 g/2 cups dark/ bittersweet chocolate, chopped
½ teaspoon sea salt flakes

To finish
50 dark/bittersweet or milk/semisweet chocolate spheres
250 g/2 cups dark/ bittersweet chocolate, tempered
4 tablespoons cocoa powder

a disposable piping/pastry bag
2 baking sheets, 1 lined with baking parchment

Makes about 50

To make the ganache, put the sugar into a small saucepan or pot set over a low heat. Add the butter and when the sugar begins to melt, add the cream and vanilla. Bring the mixture to the boil slowly, stirring until smooth.

Tip the chopped chocolate into a bowl, add the salt and pour over the hot cream. Set aside for 30 seconds to allow the chocolate to melt in the heat of the hot cream, then stir until smooth. Set aside to cool at room temperature for about 15 minutes before scooping into a disposable piping/pastry bag. Snip the end to create a nozzle/tip, pipe ganache into each truffle sphere.

Chill the truffles in the fridge for about 30 minutes to set firm.

Temper the dark/bittersweet chocolate according to the instructions on pages 20–23.

Sift the cocoa powder onto the unlined baking sheet, ready for rolling.

To finish, dip each of the filled truffles in the tempered chocolate to coat. Remove them using a dipping fork, tapping the fork on the side of the bowl to allow any excess chocolate to drip back into the bowl. Drop each truffle into the cocoa powder and roll to coat. Repeat with the remaining truffles, then transfer the coated truffles to the lined baking sheet to set firm before serving.

Lime & yuzu caramels

If there is one flavour that is going to be the number one trend this year, it's going to be yuzu – a Japanese citrus fruit (not be confused with the aniseed-flavoured Greek spirit, ouzo!). Tasting of a cross between a lime, a lemon and a mandarin, it has been used by chefs, pâtissiers and chocolatiers for a number of years now but it is becoming more readily available in both paste or liquid form so it's time to try it at home. Matched with zingy lime and creamy white chocolate, the yuzu makes its presence felt here.

250 g/1¼ cups caster/
granulated sugar
125 ml/½ cup whipping/
heavy cream
25 g/1½ tablespoons
unsalted butter
a pinch of salt
1 tablespoon yuzu juice
1 tablespoon freshly
squeezed lime juice
50 g/⅓ cup dark/
bittersweet chocolate,
melted
200 g/1½ cups white
chocolate, tempered

To garnish
grated zest of 1 lime
1 tablespoon sea salt
flakes

50 circular moulds
*2 disposable piping/pastry
bags*

Makes about 50

Begin by preparing the truffle cases. Temper the white chocolate according to the instructions on pages 20–23.

Coat the circular truffle moulds with tempered chocolate according to the instructions on pages 24–27 and let set at room temperature.

To make the caramel, tip the sugar into a large, heavy-bottomed saucepan or pot with a capacity of at least 2½ litres/11 cups – the caramel will bubble furiously in the pan later so you will need a slightly larger pan. Add 1–2 tablespoons of water and dissolve the sugar without stirring. Bring to the boil and continue to cook until the sugar becomes an amber-coloured caramel. Swirl the pan if necessary to ensure the caramel cooks evenly.

As the caramel is cooking and in a separate saucepan or pot set over a low heat, heat the cream until just boiling.

Working quickly, gradually strain the hot cream into the pan with the caramel – take care as it will splutter – and stir with a long handled wooden spoon or spatula until smooth. Add the unsalted butter and salt, and stir again until smooth. Add the yuzu and lime juice and return the pan to a low heat, simmer for 30 seconds and pour into a clean bowl to cool.

Scoop the cooled caramel into a disposable piping/pastry bag. Snip the end to create a nozzle/tip, pipe ganache into each mould.

Spoon the melted dark/bittersweet chocolate into another bag and pipe into the opening of each truffle shell to seal the caramel inside. Set in a cool, dark place until firm.

Once the ganache has set, cover the tops of the domes with more tempered white chocolate to seal according to the instructions on pages 24–27.

To garnish, rub together some the lime zest sea salt flakes. Massage the salt and lime together taking care not to break up too many of the crystals. Sprinkle a little on each truffle before serving.

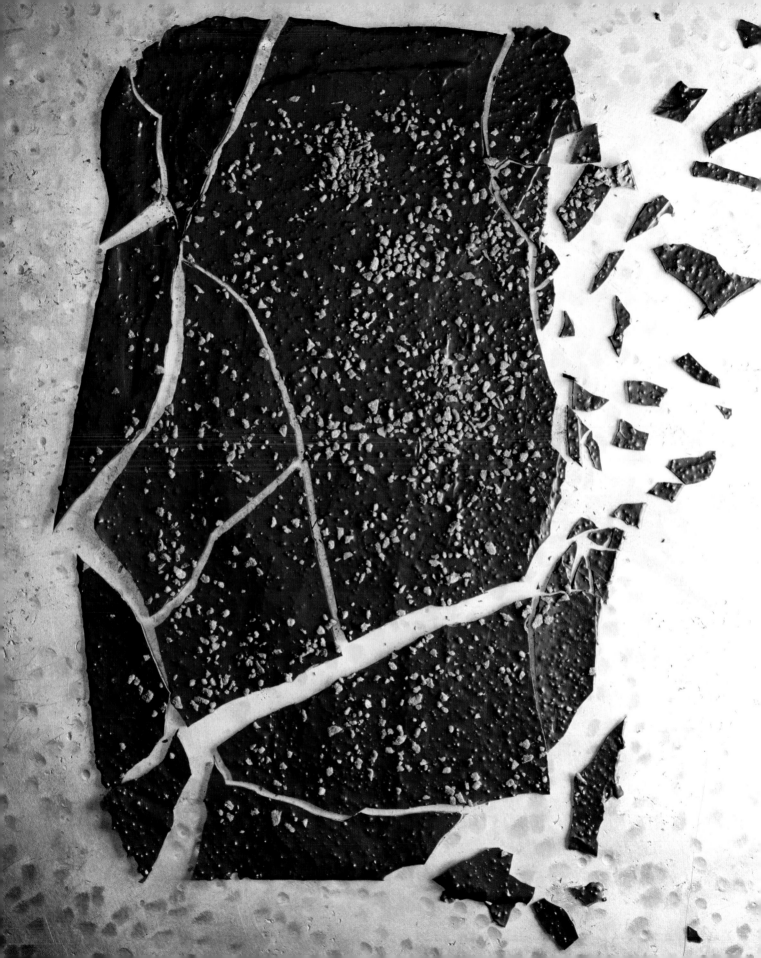

Double peppermint snap

One of the first pieces of cooking at junior school I remember doing was making peppermint creams. This is a nod to that first cooking experience, albeit an easier and more decadent version. Thin, crispy tempered chocolate mixed with demerara/turbinado sugar engulfed in peppermint extract and crystallized mint leaves sprinkled on top. I like to make it as a slab and then drop it on the table to snap into organic pieces for people to enjoy. It also works really well crumbled over vanilla ice cream.

3–4 tablespoons demerara/turbinado sugar

1–2 teaspoons peppermint extract or mint oil

250 g/2 cups dark/bittersweet chocolate

40 g/2 cups crystallized mint leaves (available online)

2 x 30 x 15-cm/12 x 6-inch baking sheets, lined with baking parchment

Serves 4–6

Mix the sugar and the peppermint extract together and set aside to infuse.

Temper the dark/bittersweet chocolate according to the instructions on pages 20–23.

Stir the peppermint-infused sugar through the tempered chocolate.

Divide the chocolate mixture between the prepared baking sheets. Sprinkle each with half of the crystallized mint leaves. Set aside at room temperature to cool completely then chill in the fridge for 30 minutes.

Create the 'snap' by lifting the set chocolate layers from the baking sheets and dropping from a height onto a clean work surface.

Variation

What's great about this recipe is that you can easily adapt the flavours you introduce. Try replacing the peppermint extract or mint oil with other essential oils, such as orange, rose, almond or coffee. The next trick is to sprinkle that same flavour on the top too, like I've done here with the crystallized mint leaves. If you substitute the mint extract for rose syrup, sprinkle crystallized rose petals across the top, and so on. You can buy a wide variety of freeze-dried fruits and zests online so experiment with the flavours you like most.

Peanut butter & raspberry jelly truffles

Who doesn't love the big and bold American flavours of peanut butter and jelly? One of my guilty pleasures is peanut butter and raspberry jam/jelly on toast so I wanted to turn a little piece of guilty pleasure into pure joy. The raspberry *pâte de fruit* replicates the jam/jelly perfectly and the peanut butter ganache makes that element even more indulgent than it already is.

Raspberry pâte de fruit
125 g/1¼ cups raspberries
freshly squeezed juice of
    ½ lemon
175 g/¾ cup plus 2
    tablespoons caster/
    granulated sugar
25 ml/1 tablespoon liquid
    pectin
½ teaspoon pure vanilla
    extract

Peanut butter ganache
125 ml/½ cup double/
    heavy cream
1 teaspoon pure vanilla
    extract
75 g/½ cup milk/
    semisweet chocolate,
    finely chopped
100 g/¾ cup dark/
    bittersweet chocolate,
    finely chopped
75 g/½ cup smooth
    unsweetened peanut
    butter
½ teaspoon sea salt flakes

To coat
250 g/2 cups dark/
    bittersweet chocolate,
    tempered
50 g/⅓ cup salted
    peanuts, finely chopped
1 tablespoon freeze-dried
    raspberry pieces

a 18-cm/7-inch square
    baking pan, greased and
    lined with clingfilm/plastic
    wrap

Makes 25–30

To make the raspberry *pâte de fruit*, put the berries in a small saucepan or pot set over a low heat with 2 teaspoons of lemon juice and 2 teaspoons of sugar. Simmer for 2–3 minutes until the raspberries soften and become juicy. Remove the pan from the heat and push the berries through a fine mesh sieve or strainer set over a bowl to remove the seeds.

Return the raspberry *pâte de fruit* to a low heat in a clean pan, add the remaining sugar and 25 ml/1 tablespoon water and stir gently to dissolve the sugar. Continue to cook steadily over a medium heat until the mixture reaches 107°C (220°F) using a sugar thermometer. Add the liquid pectin and another teaspoon of lemon juice and stir well. Continue to cook the mixture over a medium heat for 7–10 minutes, until it reaches 110–112°C (225–230°F). Simmer at this temperature for 2 minutes and then spoon ½ teaspoon of the mixture onto a cold plate and leave for 30 seconds. The *pâte de fruit* is ready when it wrinkles if pushed with the tip of your finger.

Stir the vanilla through the *pâte de fruit* and pour into the prepared baking pan. Set aside for at least 2 hours, until firm.

Meanwhile, prepare the peanut butter ganache. Pour the cream into a small saucepan or pot and add the vanilla. Set over a medium heat and bring to the boil.

Tip the finely chopped chocolates into a bowl, add the peanut butter and pour over the hot cream mixture. Set aside for 2–3 minutes to allow the chocolate to melt in the heat of the hot cream, then stir until smooth. Add the salt, stir and let cool at room temperature for 10 minutes. Pour the ganache evenly over the set *pâte de fruit*, spread level with an off-set palette knife and chill in the fridge for 1 hour.

Temper the dark/bittersweet chocolate for the coating according to the instructions on pages 20–23.

Spoon 2 tablespoons of the tempered chocolate over the top the chilled ganache and set at room temperature until firm. Lay a sheet of baking parchment over the top of the pan followed by a baking sheet, flip the pan over so that the ganache is on the bottom and the raspberry layer is on top. Lift off the pan and carefully peel off the clingfilm from the *pâte de fruit*. Using a clean, hot knife, trim the edges and cut the raspberry-topped ganache into even rectangles.

Transfer the truffles to a wire rack set over a clean baking sheet covered in baking parchment. Carefully spoon tempered chocolate over the truffles to coat. Top each truffle with a salted peanut and freeze-dried raspberry pieces and allow the chocolate to set completely before serving.

White forest fudge

Black Forest Gateau is one of my favourite cakes and when it came to writing this book, I thought it would be nice to do something with kirsch-soaked cherries and white chocolate instead of dark/bittersweet as is traditional. The late great Professor John Huber who transformed the education for pastry chefs in the UK for so many years, used to make a Swiss forest gateau which was a delicious kirsch-laden traditional black forest gateau wrapped in a collar of white chocolate, topped with cherries and a snowstorm of icing/confectioners' sugar! So here's my new take on the classic, a sweet, creamy, tangy and indulgent fudge filled with juicy kirsch-soaked cherries – delicious!

75 g/½ cup dried cherries
50 ml/¼ cup kirsch
200 g/1 cup golden caster/granulated sugar
200 g/1 cup demerara/turbinado sugar
40 g/3 tablespoons unsalted butter
1 x 170-g/6-oz. can evaporated milk
50 ml/¼ cup double/heavy cream
a pinch of salt
1 teaspoon pure vanilla extract
150 g/1¼ cups white chocolate, chopped

an 18–20-cm/7–8-inch square pan, lined with baking parchment

Makes about 40 pieces

Tip the cherries and kirsch into a small saucepan or pot set over a low heat. Gently warm the kirsch but do not allow it to boil. Stir well, remove the pan from the heat and set aside until the mixture is cold and the cherries are plump, juicy and have absorbed the kirsch.

Put both sugars, the butter, evaporated milk, cream and salt into a large, heavy-bottomed saucepan or pot with a capacity of at least 2½ litres/11 cups. Simmer over a medium heat and stir gently to dissolve the sugar. Put a sugar thermometer into the pan and bring the mixture to the boil, reduce the heat and continue to cook, without stirring, at a low, steady boil until the mixture reaches 112°C (230°F). Add the vanilla and immediately remove the pan from the heat. Set aside for a few minutes until the bubbling subsides.

Add the chopped chocolate and stir until the chocolate has melted and the mixture is smooth. Leave to cool for a further 10 minutes and then, using a wooden spoon or rubber spatula, beat the fudge until it thickens, cools and becomes slightly grainy. Add the kirsch-soaked cherries, mix to thoroughly combine. Pour the fudge into the prepared baking pan and spread level using the back of a spoon or a palette knife. Set in a cool, dark place for 3–4 hours, or overnight, until firm.

Once firm, cut the fudge into small squares before serving or store in an airtight container for up to 1 week.

Cookies, biscuits & bakes

Chocolate chip cookies

As a kid I used to make these most Saturday afternoons and then take them to school on Monday mornings. My aim was to get them just right, that is to say crunchy outside and gooey in the middle. One of my favourite desserts is warm cookies with vanilla ice cream, drizzled with maple syrup or hot chocolate sauce, or even turned into an ice cream sandwich for double the delight!

325 g/2⅔ cups plain/
all-purpose flour
½ rounded teaspoon
bicarbonate of/baking
soda
a large pinch sea salt
flakes
225 g/1 stick plus
1 tablespoon unsalted
butter, softened
100 g/½ cup caster/
granulated sugar
175 g/¾ cup plus
2 tablespoons soft light
brown sugar
2 teaspoons pure vanilla
extract
2 eggs, lightly beaten
250 g/2 cups dark/
bittersweet chocolate,
chopped into chunks

2 large baking sheets,
greased and lined with
baking parchment

Makes 20—24

Sift together the flour and bicarbonate of/baking soda into a large mixing bowl, add the salt and set aside.

Cream together the softened butter, caster/granulated and soft light brown sugar in a stand mixer for 3–5 minutes until pale and very soft. Use a rubber spatula to scrape down the sides of the mixing bowl, add the vanilla and mix again. Add the beaten eggs, a little at a time and beat until fully incorporated. Add the sifted dry ingredients and mix again to combine. Finally, fold in the chopped chocolate using a large rubber spatula or metal spoon. At this point you can bake the cookies immediately but I find that their flavour develops better if you cover and chill the cookie dough in the fridge for 24 hours.

Bring the dough to room temperature at least 30 minutes before baking.

Preheat the oven to 170°C (325°F) Gas 3.

Spoon rounded tablespoons of cookie dough onto the prepared baking sheets allowing plenty of space between each. Bake in batches on the middle shelf of the preheated oven for 10–12 minutes, until the edges of the cookies are golden brown and the middle is still slightly soft. You may need to turn the sheets around halfway through baking to ensure that the cookies brown evenly.

Allow the cookies to cool on the baking sheets for 3–4 minutes then transfer to wire racks to cool before serving.

Store the cookies in an airtight container lined with baking parchment for 4–5 days.

Variation
To make these cookies even more indulgent, pipe some ganache (see page 30) onto the bottom of one of the cookies and sandwich another cookie on top. And for even more extravagance, half dip the cookie sandwiches in tempered chocolate (see pages 22–23) and set in a cool, dark place until firm.

Macadamia & caramelized white chocolate cookies

These are the kind of cookies you want stashed away for a rainy day. They're so moreish they won't last long in the cookie jar – I always end up eating the whole batch in just one day! The white chocolate caramelizes in the oven to give lovely little bits of crunchy white chocolate that are to die for and the creamy texture of the macadamias makes a lovely contrast.

175 g/1½ sticks unsalted butter, diced

175 g/¾ cup plus 2 tablespoons soft light brown sugar

75 g/⅓ cup plus 1 tablespoon caster/granulated sugar

2 eggs, lightly beaten

1 teaspoon pure vanilla extract

250 g/2 cups plain/all-purpose flour

½ teaspoon bicarbonate of/baking soda

a pinch of sea salt flakes

150 g/1½ cups macadamia nuts, roughly chopped

275 g/2¼ cups white chocolate, roughly chopped

2 large baking sheets, greased and lined with baking parchment

Makes 25–30

Melt the butter in a small saucepan or pot set over a low–medium heat. Continue to cook for 5–10 minutes until it turns a deep golden brown colour and releases a nutty aroma. Pour the browned butter into a large mixing bowl and set aside to cool to room temperature.

Add both of the sugars to the cooled, melted butter and beat with an electric handheld whisk until pale and light. Gradually add the beaten eggs and vanilla, mixing well between each addition.

Sift the flour, bicarbonate of/baking soda and salt into the bowl and mix again to thoroughly combine. Fold in the chopped macadamia nuts and chopped chocolate.

Spoon the cookie dough onto a large sheet of baking parchment or clingfilm/plastic wrap and roll into a large sausage with a diameter of about 7 cm/3 inches. Wrap tightly and chill in the fridge for at least 1 hour or until firm.

Preheat the oven to 180°C (350°F) Gas 4.

Slice the cookie dough into discs 1-cm/⅜-inch thick, discard the baking parchment or clingfilm/plastic wrap and arrange on the prepared baking sheets allowing plenty of space between each. Bake in batches on the middle shelf of the preheated oven for 10–12 minutes, until the edges of the cookies are golden brown and the middle is still slightly soft. You may need to turn the trays around halfway through baking to ensure that the cookies brown evenly.

Allow the cookies to cool on the baking sheets for 3–4 minutes then transfer to wire racks to cool before serving.

Store the cookies in an airtight container lined with baking parchment for 4–5 days.

Milk chocolate & cardamom sablés

These sophisticated little cookies made with icing/confectioners' sugar are melt-in-the-mouth and the perfect way to end a dinner party when served with coffee or tea. The milk/semisweet chocolate works in perfect harmony with the fragrant and softly spiced cardamom sugar which crystallizes when baked to give a crisp crust to this delicate treat.

75 g/½ cup icing/
    confectioners' sugar
150 g/1 stick plus
    2 tablespoons unsalted
    butter, softened
1 vanilla bean/pod
grated zest of 1 orange
2 eggs, lightly beaten
200 g/1⅔ cups plain/
    all-purpose flour
50 g/½ cup ground
    hazelnuts
2 tablespoons cocoa
    powder
a pinch of salt
100 g/½ cup granulated/
    white sugar
6 cardamom pods, seeds
    finely ground
250 g/2 cups milk/
    semisweet chocolate

*2 large baking sheets,
    greased and lined with
    baking parchment*

Makes 25–30

Cream together the icing/confectioners' sugar and softened butter in a stand mixer for 3–5 minutes until pale and very soft.

Using a small knife split the vanilla bean in half lengthwise and scrape the seeds into the bowl with the orange zest. Stir to combine.

Gradually add the eggs, mixing well between each addition. Gently fold in the flour, ground hazelnuts, cocoa and salt using a large metal spoon, taking care not to overwork the dough as the sablés will be tough rather than crisp and light if the dough is overstretched.

Spoon the dough onto a large sheet of baking parchment or clingfilm/plastic wrap and roll into a large sausage with a diameter of about 7 cm/3 inches. Wrap tightly and chill in the fridge for at least 1 hour or until firm.

Preheat the oven to 170°C (325°F) Gas 3.

Mix the granulated/white sugar with the finely ground cardamom seeds and tip onto an unlined baking sheet. Unwrap the chilled sablé dough and roll the sausage in the cardamom sugar to coat evenly. Using a sharp knife cut the dough into discs, each about 4-mm/⅛-inch thick and arrange on the prepared baking sheets.

Bake in batches on the middle shelf of the preheated oven for 10–15 minutes, until crisp.

Allow the sablés to cool on the baking sheets for 3–4 minutes then transfer to wire racks to cool completely.

Temper the milk/semisweet chocolate according to the instructions on pages 20–23.

Dip the underside of each cooled sablé in the tempered chocolate and transfer to a clean sheet of baking parchment to set before serving.

Store the sablés in an airtight container lined with baking parchment for 4–5 days.

Roasted cacao nib & lavender tuile shards

When I'm decorating desserts such as the Apricot & Rosemary Délice (page 119), a simple tuile placed on top can be the perfect finishing touch. The cacao nibs give a wonderful burst of intensely rich cocoa, followed nicely by the classic flavour of lavender, which has long been a well-loved partner to chocolate.

75 g/5 tablespoons unsalted butter

1 tablespoon golden/light corn syrup

100 g/$\frac{1}{2}$ cup caster/ granulated sugar

35 g/$\frac{1}{4}$ cup plain/ all-purpose flour

a pinch of salt

1 tablespoon dried lavender

50 g/$\frac{2}{3}$ cup cocoa nibs

2 large baking sheets, greased and lined with baking parchment

Makes about 20

Melt the butter with the golden/light corn syrup in a small saucepan or pot set over a low–medium heat.

Tip the sugar, flour, salt, dried lavender and cocoa nibs into a bowl and mix well to combine. Pour over the hot butter mixture and beat until smooth. Set the mixture aside at room temperature to rest for 1 hour.

Preheat the oven to 170°C (325°F) Gas 3.

Spoon 3 or 4 cherry-sized balls of mixture onto each prepared baking sheet and spread out as thinly as you can, using an off-set palette knife. Bake on the middle shelf of the preheated oven for 6–8 minutes, or until golden brown and bubbling.

Remove from the oven and set aside to cool for 30 seconds, then carefully lift off the sheet with a palette knife and wrap around a lightly-oiled rolling pin to create a curled tuile biscuit shape. Leave until crisp before carefully removing the tuile from the rolling pin. Repeat with the remaining baked dough.

These delicate crisp biscuits do not like damp or humidity – it will soften them – so make them on the day you plan to serve them. Cool and store in an airtight container after baking.

Cherry & almond 'bourbons'

When people ask what my favourite cookie is, I always say bourbon biscuits, mainly because they are full of chocolate, but also because as a child I remember taking the cookie apart and eating the filling first. My take on this classic treat is to combine it with another much-loved dessert, the bakewell tart. Here cherry jam/jelly is surrounded by a ganache flavoured with almond liqueur to create a flavour combination that is instantly recognisable as the classic bakewell.

Cookies

225 g/2 sticks unsalted butter, at room temperature
125 g/scant 1 cup icing/confectioners' sugar
1 teaspoon pure vanilla extract
2 egg yolks
270 g/2 cups plus 1 tablespoon plain/all-purpose flour, plus extra for rolling out
30 g/¼ cup cocoa powder

Filling

100 g/¾ cup dark/bittersweet chocolate (70%), finely chopped
50 ml/¼ cup whipping/heavy cream
1 tablespoon Amaretto di Saronno or other almond liqueur
1–2 teaspoons pure almond extract
1 teaspoon unsalted butter, softened
1 x 340-g/12-oz. jar cherry jam/jelly

2 large baking sheets, greased and lined with baking parchment
an 7 x 4 cm/2¾ x 1½-inch 'EAT ME' cookie cutter or similar
a piping/pastry bag fitted with a plain nozzle/tip

Makes 18

To make the cookie dough, cream the butter and sugar together until pale and light using an electric handheld whisk. Add the vanilla and mix again. Then add the egg yolks, one at a time, mixing well between each addition and scraping down the side of the bowl with a rubber spatula. Sift in the flour and cocoa powder and beat until smooth.

Turn out the dough onto a lightly floured work surface and bring it together, forming a ball with your hands. Wrap in clingfilm/plastic wrap, flatten into a disc and chill for at least 4 hours or until needed.

Preheat the oven to 170°C (325°F) Gas 3.

Roll out half of the dough to a thickness of about 2 mm/⅛ inch on a lightly floured surface. Using the cutter, stamp out as many cookies as you can from the dough and arrange on the prepared baking sheets. Gather the scraps together and set aside while you roll out the remaining dough. Stamp out and arrange the cookies, as before, then lightly knead all the scraps together, roll again and cut out as many cookies as you can.

Chill the cookies on the sheets in the fridge for 10–15 minutes, then bake on the middle shelves of the preheated oven for about 12 minutes, or until crisp. Remove from the oven and let the cookies cool slightly on the baking sheets for 3–4 minutes before transferring them to a wire rack to cool completely.

To make the filling, tip the chopped chocolate into a heatproof bowl set over a saucepan or pot of barely simmering water. Add the cream, Amaretto, almond extract and butter, and heat for about 3 minutes. Stir gently until the chocolate has melted and the mixture is smooth. Remove from the heat and set aside to cool.

Scoop the filling into a piping/pastry bag fitted with the plain nozzle/tip. Turn half of the cookies so that they are writing side down and pipe the filling in a border around each cookie leaving a clear space in the middle.

Spoon cherry jam/jelly into the centre of each piped cookie, then top with the remaining plain cookies and gently press together. These are best enjoyed straightaway.

White chocolate & passion fruit 'custard creams'

Who doesn't love custard creams? Again, like my love for bourbons, I always eat the filling first and then dunk the cookie into my tea. The sweetness of the white chocolate cuts through the astringent beauty of the passion fruit and the addition of passion fruit powder boosts the flavour nicely.

Cookies

200 g/1 stick plus
   5 tablespoons unsalted
   butter, softened
125 g/scant 1 cup icing/
   confectioners' sugar
1 teaspoon pure vanilla
   extract
2 eggs, lightly beaten
300 g/2⅓ cups plain/
   all-purpose flour, plus
   extra for rolling out
½ teaspoon baking
   powder
50 g/½ cup custard/
   instant pudding
   powder
30 g/2 tablespoons
   freeze-dried passion
   fruit powder
a pinch of salt

Buttercream

125 g/1 cup white
   chocolate, chopped
2 large passionfruit, flesh
   scooped out and skins
   discarded
125 g/1 stick plus
   1 tablespoon unsalted
   butter, softened
70 g/scant ¾ cup icing/
   confectioners' sugar
½ teaspoon pure vanilla
   extract
1 teaspoon freeze-dried
   passion fruit powder

2 large baking sheets,
   greased and lined with
   baking parchment
a heart-shaped WITH LOVE
   cookie cutter or similar,
   about 7 cm/2¾ inches
   diameter

Makes 18

To make the cookie dough, cream the butter and sugar together until pale and light using an electric handheld whisk. Add the vanilla and mix again. Then add the beaten eggs, a little at a time, mixing well between each addition and scraping down the side of the bowl with a rubber spatula. Sift in the flour baking powder, custard powder, passion fruit powder and salt, and beat until smooth.

Turn out the dough onto a lightly floured work surface and bring it together, forming a ball with your hands. Wrap in clingfilm/plastic wrap, flatten into a disc and chill for at least 4 hours or until needed.

Preheat the oven to 170°C (325°F) Gas 3.

Roll out half of the dough to a thickness of about 2 mm/⅛ inch on a lightly floured surface. Using the cutter, stamp out as many cookies as you can from the dough and arrange on the prepared baking sheets. Gather the scraps together and set aside while you roll out the remaining dough. Stamp out and arrange the cookies, as before, then lightly knead all the scraps together, roll again and cut out as many cookies as you can.

Bake on the middle shelves of the preheated oven for about 12 minutes, or until crisp.

Remove from the oven and let the cookies cool slightly on the baking sheets for 3–4 minutes before transferring them to a wire rack to cool completely.

To make the buttercream, melt the chocolate in a heatproof bowl set over a saucepan or pot of barely simmering water. Heat for about 3 minutes. Stir gently until the chocolate has melted and the mixture is smooth. Remove from the heat and set aside to cool.

Press the passion fruit pulp and juice through a fine mesh sieve or strainer set over a bowl, discarding the black seeds. You should have 3–4 tablespoons of pulp.

Cream together the butter with the sugar, vanilla, passion fruit pulp and passion fruit powder using a handheld electric whisk, until smooth and very light. Add the cooled white chocolate and mix again until combined.

Spread the underside of half of the cookies with the buttercream, then top with the remaining cookies. Store in an airtight container lined with baking parchment for 2–3 days.

Hazelnut, apricot & chocolate 'jammy dodgers'

Cookies
100 g/1 cup blanched hazelnuts
225 g/2 sticks unsalted butter, softened
150 g/¾ cups caster/superfine sugar
1 teaspoon pure vanilla extract
3 egg yolks
250 g/2 cups plain/all-purpose flour, plus extra for rolling out
½ teaspoon baking powder
25 g/2 tablespoons cocoa powder
a pinch of salt

Filling
50 g/¼ cup caster/granulated sugar
50 g/½ cup blanched hazelnuts
100 g/¾ cup dark/bittersweet chocolate (65–70%), finely chopped
3 tablespoons double/heavy cream
2 tablespoons condensed milk
apricot jam/jelly
icing/confectioners' sugar, to dust

a 6-cm/2½-inch and a 3-cm/1¼-inch round cookie cutter
2 baking sheets, greased and lined with baking parchment
a disposable piping/pastry bag

Makes 24–30

As a kid, I always used to wonder how they got the jam/jelly inside the little circle of a jammy dodger, without the jam coming out the sides and now I know. I've played around with another classic here, by filling it with apricot preserve and a homemade nutty chocolate spread. Both are also delicious spread on hot toast or a warm croissant.

To make the cookie dough, finely grind the hazelnuts in a food processor and set aside. Cream the butter, sugar and vanilla together until pale and light using an electric handheld whisk. Add the egg yolks, one at a time, mixing well between each addition and scraping down the side of the bowl with a rubber spatula. Sift in the flour, ground hazelnuts, baking powder, cocoa powder and salt, and beat until smooth. Do not overwork the dough otherwise the cookies will be tough and not crisp and light.

Turn out the dough onto a lightly floured work surface and Lightly knead, bringing it together to form a ball with your hands. Wrap in clingfilm/plastic wrap, flatten into a disc and chill for at least 1 hour, or until needed.

Preheat the oven to 170°C (325°F) Gas 3.

Roll out half of the dough to a thickness of about 2 mm/⅛ inch on a lightly floured surface. Using the larger cutter, stamp out as many cookies as you can from the dough and arrange on the prepared baking sheets. Roll out the remaining dough and repeat. Gather the scraps together and lightly knead them, roll again and cut out as many more cookies as you can. Use the smaller cutter to cut holes from the middle of half of the cookies. Chill in the fridge for 15 minutes and then bake on the middle shelves of the preheated oven for about 12–15 minutes, or until crisp.

To make the filling, tip the sugar into a small saucepan or pot set over a low heat. Add 1 tablespoon of water, and dissolve the sugar without stirring. Bring to the boil and continue to cook the syrup until it becomes an amber-coloured caramel.

Remove the pan from the heat and slowly add the hazelnuts. Stir well to coat, then pour the mixture onto a sheet of baking parchment. Set aside until completely cool and finely grind in a food processor until the praline has become slightly runny and the nuts are almost smooth.

Melt the dark/bittersweet chocolate according to the instructions on page 20.

Add the melted chocolate to the food processor with the ground praline. Pour in the cream and condensed/evaporated milk, add the salt, and whizz until silky smooth.

Scoop the filling into a disposable piping/pastry bag. Snip the end to create a nozzle/tip, the pipe the filling in a border around each whole cookie. Spoon the apricot jam/jelly into the centre of each whole cookie.

Dust the cookies with holes in the centre with icing/confectioners' sugar, then top the dressed whole cookies and very gently press them together. These are best enjoyed straightaway.

Maple & pecan brownies

The humble brownie has escalated in years gone by into the must-have product in any and every café, pâtisserie or restaurant. I think we love it because it is just so versatile as a dessert – enjoy it hot with ice cream, chilled and fudgy from the fridge, topped with ganache or simply dusted with icing/confectioners' sugar or cocoa powder. And best of all there isn't that much washing up at the end!

150 g/1½ cups pecans
175 g/½ cup maple syrup
225 g/1⅔ cups dark/ bittersweet chocolate, chopped
150 g/1 stick plus 2 tablespoons unsalted butter
150 g/¾ cup soft dark brown sugar
3 large eggs, beaten
1 teaspoon pure vanilla extract
a large pinch sea salt flakes
125 g/⅔ cup plain/ all-purpose flour

a 20 x 30-cm/8 x 12-inch baking pan, greased and lined with buttered baking parchment

Makes 16–20 squares

Preheat the oven to 180°C (350°F) Gas 4.

Tip the pecans onto the prepared baking sheet, drizzled with 30 g/2 tablespoons of the maple syrup. Toast the nuts on the middle shelf of the preheated oven for 6–8 minutes until crisp and starting to caramelize. Remove from the oven and set aside for 3–4 minutes to cool, then roughly chop.

Melt the chocolate and butter in a heatproof bowl set over a saucepan or pot of simmering water. Stir until smooth, remove from the heat and leave to cool slightly for 2–3 minutes.

Mix the sugar and remaining maple syrup into the melted chocolate mixture and stir until silky smooth. Add the eggs, vanilla and salt. Mix again to combine, taking care not to over beat the mixture.

Sift in the flour and fold in, using either a rubber spatula or large metal spoon. Stir through half of the caramelized pecans, then pour the mixture into the prepared baking pan. Scatter with the remaining caramelized pecans.

Bake on the middle shelf of the preheated oven for 25 minutes, until the top has a light crust but the middle is still soft to the touch.

Remove from the oven and set aside to cool before cutting into squares to serve.

The brownies will keep in an airtight container for up to 1 week.

Cranberry & white chocolate blondies

Blondies are basically brownies made with white chocolate. I like to add ground almonds to help with the texture of them and the cranberries to cut through the sweetness of the white chocolate. Finished with an extra drizzle of white chocolate and sprinkled with freeze-dried cranberries, these make an irresistible dessert and can be kept in the fridge overnight if you have any left over.

175 g/1½ sticks unsalted butter, diced

175 g/1⅓ cups white chocolate, finely chopped

125 g/⅔ cup caster/granulated sugar

75 g/generous ⅓ cup light muscovado sugar

3 eggs

1 teaspoon pure vanilla extract

125 g/⅔ cup plain/all-purpose flour

75 g/¾ cup ground almonds

½ teaspoon baking powder

a pinch of salt

75 g/½ cup white chocolate chips

100 g/⅔ cup dried cranberries

50 g/⅔ cup flaked/slivered almonds

To finish

75–100 g/½–¾ cup white chocolate, chopped

1 tablespoon freeze-dried cranberry powder (optional)

20 x 30-cm/8 x 12-inch baking pan, greased and lined with baking parchment

Makes 16–20

Preheat the oven to 180°C (350°F) Gas 4.

Melt the butter in a heatproof bowl set over a saucepan or pot of simmering water. Add the chopped white chocolate, remove from the heat and stir occasionally until all the chocolate has melted.

Tip the caster/granulated and light muscovado sugars into a large mixing bowl with the eggs. Whisk with a handheld electric whisk for about 5 minutes, until pale, light and the mixture holds a ribbon trail. Add the vanilla and whisk again. Pour the butter and white chocolate mixture into the bowl and mix briefly to combine. Sift in the plain flour, ground almonds, baking powder and salt, and mix gently. Fold in the white chocolate chips and dried cranberries.

Spoon the mixture into the prepared baking pan, spread level and scatter with flaked/slivered almonds.

Bake on the middle shelf of the preheated oven for 30 minutes, until the top has a light crust but the middle is still soft to the touch. Remove from the oven and set aside to cool

Melt the remaining white chocolate in a heatproof bowl set over a saucepan or pot of simmering water. Stir until smooth, remove from the heat and cool slightly.

Drizzle the melted white chocolate over the top of the blondies, from a height. Set aside for 10 minutes and then sprinkle with freeze-dried cranberry powder, if using. Cut into squares to serve.

The blondies will keep in an airtight container for up to 1 week.

Nans' chocolate fudge cake

So this is my baking inspiration and one of my first, vivid food memories. Nans used to make this cake for my sister's birthday and my birthday every year and it never failed to disappoint. It is relatively simple to make, but every time I make it now, I am instantly transported back to her small kitchen and not quite reaching the top of the worktop, but always wanting to beat the batter, lick the spoon and of course make the icing and decorate with chocolate buttons. Sorry Nans, I couldn't bring myself to put chocolate buttons on top of this one, but I hope you like the shavings – it brings back so many wonderful memories.

Cake
- 50 g/⅓ cup cocoa powder
- 200 g/1 stick plus 5 tablespoons unsalted butter, softened
- 150 g/¾ cup caster/superfine sugar
- 125 g/scant ⅔ cup soft light brown sugar
- 4 eggs
- 1 teaspoon pure vanilla extract
- 250 g/2 cups plain/all-purpose flour
- 1½ teaspoons baking powder
- ½ teaspoon bicarbonate of/baking soda
- a pinch of salt
- 4 tablespoons whole milk

Frosting
- 100 g/¾ cup dark/bittersweet chocolate, chopped
- 200 g/1 stick plus 5 tablespoons unsalted butter, softened
- 225 g/1¾ cups icing/confectioners' sugar
- 2 tablespoons cocoa powder, sifted
- 2 tablespoons golden/light corn syrup
- 2 tablespoons whole milk
- 1 teaspoon pure vanilla extract

chocolate shavings, cocoa or chocolate sprinkles

2 x 20-cm/8-inch round cake pans, greased and lined with baking parchment

Serves 8

Preheat the oven to 180°C (350°F) Gas 4.

Combine the cocoa powder with 5 tablespoons of boiling water in a small bowl and mix to a smooth paste.

Cream the softened butter with both sugars, using an electric handheld whisk for 3–4 minutes, until pale and light. Scrape down the bowl with a rubber spatula, add the eggs, one at a time, mixing well between each addition. Add the vanilla and mix again until combined.

Sift in the flour, baking powder, bicarbonate of/baking soda and salt. Add the cocoa paste and milk, and beat until thoroughly combined.

Divide the mixture evenly between the prepared baking pans and spread level with a palette knife.

Bake on the middle shelves of the preheated oven for about 25 minutes, or until a knife inserted into the cakes comes out clean.

Remove from the oven and set the cakes aside in their pans on top of a wire rack to cool for 5 minutes. Remove the cakes from the pans, peel off the baking parchment and allow to cool completely.

To make the frosting, melt the chocolate in a heatproof bowl set over a saucepan or pot of barely simmering water. Stir until smooth, remove from the heat and set aside to cool slightly. Beat the butter until pale, light and creamy, and then gradually add the icing/confectioners' sugar 1 tablespoon at a time, scraping down the sides of the bowl as you go. Add the cocoa powder, golden/light corn syrup, milk and vanilla, and mix until smooth. Add the cooled, melted chocolate and mix again until smooth.

To assemble, place one of the cakes on a serving plate and cover with 3 tablespoons of frosting, smoothing with a palette knife. Top with the second cake, gently pressing the two cakes together.

Cover the top of the cake with the remaining frosting and scatter the chocolate shavings or or sprinkles over the top before serving.

Milk chocolate, prune & armagnac stollen

175 g/generous 1 cup
pitted prunes

freshly squeezed juice and
grated zest of 1 orange

4 tablespoons Armagnac
or other brandy

2 teaspoons mixed/apple
pie spice

75 g/scant 1 cup flaked/
slivered almonds

150 g/1¼ cups dark/
bittersweet chocolate
chips

500 g/4 cups strong/bread
flour, plus extra for
rolling out

½ teaspoon sea salt

50 g/¼ cup caster/
superfine sugar

40 g/3 tablespoons soft
light brown sugar

a 10-g/⅓-oz. packet fast-
action dried yeast

3 eggs, lightly beaten

125 ml/½ cup whole milk

continued overleaf

When Christmas comes around every year, I always think, 'I should make presents this year, like jams/jellies or biscuits/cookies', but never get round to doing it. So this year, I made a big batch of stollen – a classic German sweet bread, flavoured with festive spices and lots of glacé cherries or dried fruits – but with prunes soaked in Armagnac and milk chocolate in a tear-and-share wreath instead of the classic loaf. The batch made two so I ate one with my family and wrapped the second in baking parchment and gave it to a friend! Maybe I'll get round to making that jam next year…

Roughly chop or snip the prunes and tip into a bowl with the orange juice and grated zest, Armagnac, spice, almonds and chocolate chips. Mix well, cover and leave overnight for the prunes to absorb the liquid. **(A)**

The next day tip the flour into the bowl of a stand mixer fitted with a dough hook. Add the salt, sugar, yeast, eggs, milk, vanilla and 125 g/6 tablespoons of the softened butter. Mix on a low speed to combine the ingredients into a rough dough. **(B)**

Continue to mix for a further 4–5 minutes until the dough is silky smooth, elastic and comes

away cleanly from the side of the bowl. Add the prune mixture and mix again until combined – about 2 minutes. Cover the bowl with clingfilm/plastic wrap and leave in the fridge overnight until almost doubled in size.

The next day, bring the dough out of the fridge and bring back to room temperature. Dust the work surface with flour, tip the dough out of the bowl and knead the dough for 30 seconds – it will be quite sticky. Divide the dough into two even pieces. Roll one piece out into a rectangle roughly 40 x 15 cm/ 16 x 6 inches. **(C)**

D

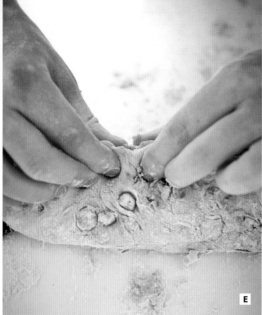

E

F

2 teaspoons pure vanilla extract

150 g/1 stick plus 2 tablespoons unsalted butter, softened

500 g/1 lb./1¾ cups marzipan

3 rounded tablespoons icing/confectioners' sugar

2 large baking sheets, greased and lined with baking parchment

Makes 2 stollen, each serving 12

Roll half of the marzipan into a 35-cm/14-inch sausage. Lay the marzipan down the middle of the dough rectangle and fold the dough up and over the marzipan to completely and neatly encase it. The seam should be on the underside. (D, E)

Transfer the roll to one of the prepared baking sheets. Shape the marzipan-filled dough into a ring roughly 25 cm/10 inches in diameter and press the ends together to seal. Repeat with the second piece of dough and marzipan. Loosely cover the stollen with clingfilm/plastic wrap and leave to prove in a warm draught-free spot for a couple of hours.

Repeat with the second piece of rolled dough and remaining marzipan.

Preheat the oven to 180°C (350°F) Gas 4.

Using a baker's blade, scissors or sharp knife slash the top of the stollens at regular intervals. (F)

Bake in the middle of the preheated oven for 15–20 minutes and then reduce the temperature to 150°C (300°F) Gas 3 and cook for a further 15 minutes until golden brown. Swap the sheets around half way through baking.

Leave the stollen to cool for 10 minutes and then melt the remaining butter in a small saucepan. Brush the top and sides of each stollen with butter and then liberally dust with icing/confectioners' sugar. Leave to cool completely on a wire rack before serving.

Crumble

**50 g/scant ½ cup plain/
all-purpose flour**

**50 g/½ cup ground
almonds**

**50 g/¼ cup caster/
granulated sugar**

**50 g/3½ tablespoons
unsalted butter, chilled
and diced**

Cake

**150 g/1¼ cups white
chocolate, chopped**

**200 g/1 stick plus
6 tablespoons
unsalted butter**

4 eggs

**100 g/½ cup caster/
superfine sugar**

**100 g/½ cup light brown
sugar**

**2 teaspoons ground
cinnamon**

**1 teaspoon pure vanilla
extract**

**150 g/1 cup plus
2 tablespoons self-
raising/rising flour**

**100 g/1 cup ground
hazelnuts or almonds**

Buttercream

**50 g/2 oz/⅓ cup chopped
white chocolate**

**175 g/1⅓ cups caster/
granulated sugar**

3 egg whites

a pinch of salt

**1 teaspoon pure vanilla
extract**

**250 g/2 sticks plus
1 tablespoon unsalted
butter, softened**

**4–5 tablespoons
blackcurrant jam/jelly**

*2 x 20-cm/8-inch round
sandwich pans, greased
and lined with baking
parchment*

Serves 8

Spiced white chocolate & blackcurrant crumble cake

This is my seasonal, winter warming version of a classic Victoria sponge cake. I add a collection of spices and white chocolate and then bake it with a buttery crumble on top that adds loads of texture and gives a good, old-fashioned British crumble feel. Filled with juicy blackcurrant jam/jelly and white chocolate buttercream – it really is extremely decadent.

Preheat the oven to 170°C (325°F) Gas 3.

Prepare the crumble first. Tip all of the ingredients into the bowl of a food processor and pulse until the butter has been rubbed into the dry ingredients and the mixture starts to clump together.

To make the cake, melt the chocolate and butter together in a heatproof bowl either over a saucepan of simmering water or in the microwave on a low setting. Stir until smooth and remove from the heat. Put the eggs, both sugars, cinnamon and vanilla extract into the bowl of a stand mixer and whisk on high for 5–10 minutes, until the mixture is doubled in size, light and foamy, and will hold a ribbon trail when the whisk is lifted from the bowl.

Pour the melted chocolate and butter into the beaten egg mixture and using a large metal spoon or rubber spatula, gently mix until thoroughly combined. Sift the flour and ground almonds over the mixture and fold in until smooth. Divide the batter evenly between the prepared cake pans, even the surface with a palette knife and sprinkle the crumble mixture on top. Bake on the middle shelf of the preheated oven for 25–30 minutes, until well risen and golden brown, and a skewer comes out clean when pushed into the middle of the cakes.

Leave the cakes to cool in the pans resting on a wire rack for 5 minutes and then carefully lift out onto the rack and let cool completely.

To make the buttercream, melt the white chocolate in a heatproof bowl over a pan of simmering water or in short bursts on a low setting in the microwave. Set aside. Put the egg whites, 2 tablespoons of the sugar and a pinch of salt into the bowl of a stand mixer and begin whisking. Tip the remaining sugar into a small pan, add 50 ml/scant ¼ cup water and bring to the boil. Pop a sugar thermometer into the pan and cook until the syrup reaches 121°C/250°F.

Once the syrup has reached the right temperature, slide off the heat and slowly pour over the meringue, whisking constantly. Continue to whisk until the meringue is stiff, glossy and the bowl is cold. Add the vanilla and, whisking constantly, add the butter, one tablespoon at a time. Finally add the melted chocolate – the mixture should be shiny.

To assemble, place one cake layer on a serving plate, crumble-side uppermost and spread with half of the buttercream. Carefully top the buttercream with the blackcurrant jam. Cover the second cake layer with the remaining buttercream and gently place on top of the first cake.

A

B

Cake

40 g/⅓ cup cocoa powder

150 g/1 stick plus
   2 tablespoons unsalted
   butter, softened

100 g/½ cup caster/
   superfine sugar

125 g/scant ⅔ cup soft
   light brown sugar

3 eggs

1 teaspoon pure vanilla
   extract

200 g/1⅔ cups plain/
   all-purpose flour

1 teaspoon baking
   powder

½ teaspoon bicarbonate
   of/baking soda

a pinch of salt

3 tablespoons whole milk

Rum syrup

100 g/¾ cup caster/
   granulated sugar

2–3 tablespoons dark rum

Rum ganache

75 g/½ cup milk/
   semisweet chocolate,
   chopped

175 g/1⅓ cups dark/
   bittersweet chocolate,
   chopped

225 ml/scant 1 cup
   double/heavy cream

1 tablespoon soft light
   brown sugar

15 g/1 tablespoon
   unsalted butter

3 tablespoons dark rum

a pinch of salt

continued overleaf

Salted caramel & rum top hat cake

If you're looking for a centrepiece celebration cake then look no further – here it is! These trendy, taller but smaller cakes are here to stay. The fillings are piped in rings, creating a lovely finish when you cut into the cake. Finish as elaborately as you like, but caramel, rum and chocolate – yes please!

Preheat the oven to 180°C (350°F) Gas 4.

In a small bowl, mix the cocoa powder with 4 tablespoons boiling water, until smooth.

Cream the softened butter with both sugars in a stand mixer for 3–4 minutes, until pale and light. Scrape down the bowl with a rubber spatula, add the eggs one at a time, mixing well between each addition. Add the vanilla extract and mix again until combined.

Sift the flour, baking powder, bicarbonate of/baking soda and a pinch of salt into the bowl. Add the cocoa paste and milk, and beat again until smooth and thoroughly combined. Divide the mixture between the cake pans and spread level with a palette knife.

Bake on the middle shelf of the preheated oven for about 35 minutes, or until a skewer inserted into the cakes comes out clean. Cool the cakes in the pans sitting on a wire rack for 5 minutes, then turn out of the pans, peel off the baking parchment and leave to cool completely.

To make the rum syrup, tip all of the ingredients into a small saucepan filled with 100 ml/scant ½ cup water and bring slowly to the boil to dissolve the sugar. Simmer for 2 minutes, until slightly thickened. Remove from the heat and leave to cool.

When the cakes are cold, use a long serrated knife to slice the rounded tops off the cakes, to make each the same height and level. (A)

Caramel buttercream
**200 g/1 stick plus
5 tablespoons unsalted
butter, softened**
**1 x 397-g/14-oz. can
ready-made caramel,
such as Carnation**
**1 tablespoon icing/
confectioners' sugar**
a pinch of salt

Chocolate glaze
**100 ml/⅓ cup whipping/
heavy cream**
1 tablespoon liquid glucose
**20 g/1½ tablespoons
unsalted butter**
**125 g/1 cup dark/
bittersweet chocolate**
**80 g/⅔ cup milk/
semisweet chocolate**

To decorate
cocoa nibs
edible gold dust and leaf

*2 x 15-cm/6-inch round cake
pan, greased and base-
lined with baking
parchment*
*2 disposable piping/pastry
bags*

Serves 8–10

Slice each cake in half horizontally to make 4 layers of even thickness. Brush the top of each layer generously with rum syrup. **(B, page 101)**

To make the ganache, combine the chopped chocolates in a bowl and set aside. Heat the cream, soft light brown sugar, rum, and a pinch of salt in a small saucepan until just boiling, pour over the chopped chocolate, stir briefly and set aside for 3 minutes for the chocolate to melt in the heat of the hot cream. Stir until silky smooth and then leave the ganache until cold and firm enough to pipe – about 3–4 hours at cool room temperature.

To make the caramel buttercream, place the softened butter, caramel, icing/confectioners' sugar and salt in a stand mixer and beat until really smooth. Keep it in the mixer until you need it as it will set too much if you put it in a piping/pastry bag now.

Fill one piping/pastry bag with two thirds of the caramel buttercream and the other with two thirds of the rum ganache. Snip the ends into 1-cm/⅜-inch wide nozzles.

Lay 3 of the cake layers on the work surface and pipe a neat 1-cm/⅜-inch wide ring of

ganache on the top of each cake as close to the outsides edge of each cake as possible. Pipe a ring of caramel buttercream inside this. Repeat this alternate piping until the top of the cake is completely covered in frosting in neat rings. **(C)**

Stack the frosted cake layers together and top with the fourth unfrosted layer. Gently press the cakes together. **(D)**

Using a palette knife, spread some of the reserved caramel buttercream in a smooth, thin layer around the outside of the cakes, and chill for 15 minutes. Spread the remaining buttercream over the top and sides of the cake using a palette knife to create a totally smooth surface. Chill the cake for 20 minutes. **(E)**

Tip all of the glaze ingredients into a small saucepan set over a low heat. Stir until smooth, then remove from the heat and cool. Place the cake on a wire rack with a baking tray underneath. Pour the glaze over the top and sides of the cake to coat smoothly. **(F)**

Press cocoa nibs around the bottom of the cake. Decorate the top with more cocoa nibs and edible gold dust and leaf and serve.

Chocolate angel cake

Chocolate cakes have a bad reputation for always being rich and filling but this lighter-than-air angel cake sets the record straight. Lightly tickled with cocoa powder, it works really well baked in a bundt pan or kugelhopf pan to give you a dramatic finish, which could be enhanced with a drizzle of chocolate glaze. For me, it's perfect as it is and a delicious coffee or tea time treat.

250 g/1¼ cups caster/ superfine sugar

100 g/½ cup plain/ all-purpose flour

35 g/¼ cup cocoa powder

½ teaspoon baking powder

10 egg whites

½ teaspoon cream of tartar

a pinch of salt

1 teaspoon pure vanilla extract

50 g/⅓ cup dark/ bittersweet chocolate, coarsely grated

icing/confectioners' sugar, to dust

Chocolate glaze (optional)

100 ml/⅓ cup whipping/ heavy cream

1 tablespoon liquid glucose

20 g/1½ tablespoons unsalted butter

125 g/1 cup dark/ bittersweet chocolate

80 g/½ cup milk/ semisweet chocolate

a 26 x 9½-cm/10 x 3-inch bundt/kugelhopf pan, greased and lightly dusted with flour

Serves 12

Preheat the oven to 180°C (350°F) Gas 4.

Sift half the sugar together with the flour, cocoa and baking powder onto a sheet of baking parchment.

Tip the egg whites into the bowl of a stand mixer fitted with a whisk attachment. Add the cream of tartar and salt, and whisk on medium speed until the egg whites will hold a firm but not dry peak. Gradually add the remaining sugar, 1 tablespoon at a time, whisking well between each addition. Add the vanilla extract and continue to whisk until the mixture is stiff and glossy.

At this stage you may find it easier to tip the mixture into a larger mixing bowl if you have one. Add the sifted dry ingredients and the grated chocolate, then, using a large metal spoon, fold into the egg whites using a figure of 8 action, until the batter is smooth and the dry ingredients are thoroughly incorporated.

Spoon the mixture into the cake pan, run a knife through the batter and sharply tap the pan on the work surface to knock out any large air bubbles. Bake in the middle of the preheated oven for 35 minutes, until well risen, springy and a skewer comes out of the cake clean.

Turn the cake pan upside down onto a cooling rack and leave to cool in the inverted pan for 1 hour or until completely cold. Loosen the edges of the cake with a small palette knife and then turn the cake out of the pan onto the cooling rack.

If you would like to add a glaze, tip all of the glaze ingredients into a small saucepan or pot and set over a low heat to melt. Stir constantly until smooth, then remove from the heat and let cool slightly.

To finish either dust the cake with icing/ confectioners' sugar or spoon the glaze over.

Hot pepper cake with chilli ganache

Chocolate and chilli/chile is one of those combinations you just can't ignore. I've given it a different new twist by using a hot pepper sauce and topping the cake with slithers of candied chilli/chile. It's not for the faint-hearted, but sure does pack a punch in the flavour territory. Try making it with hot piri piri sauce for something completely different. Go on, add as much as your dare!

Cake
250 g/2 cups plain/ all-purpose flour, plus extra for dusting
65 g/²⁄₃ cup cocoa powder, plus extra for dusting
100 g/¾ cup dark/ bittersweet chocolate, chopped
1 teaspoon baking powder
1 teaspoon sea salt
350 g/1¼ cups demerara/ turbinado sugar
3 large eggs, lightly beaten
250 ml/1 cup extra virgin olive oil
2 teaspoons Tabasco/hot pepper sauce, plus extra for the ganache
1 teaspoon pure vanilla extract

Ganache
350 g/3 cups dark/ bittersweet chocolate (70%), chopped
175 ml/¾ cup double/ heavy cream
25 g/1½ tablespoons unsalted butter
1 rounded tablespoon light brown sugar

Garnish
1 red chilli/chile
2 tablespoons caster/ granulated sugar

a 20-cm/8-inch springform cake pan, greased and lined with baking parchment
baking sheet, lined with baking parchment

Serves 6–8

Preheat the oven to 180°C (350°F) Gas 4.

Mix together 2 teaspoons of plain/all-purpose flour and cocoa and use to dust the inside of the lined cake pan, tapping out the excess.

Melt the chocolate in a heatproof bowl over a pan of barely simmering water. Stir until smooth, then remove from the heat and let cool slightly.

In a large bowl sift together the remaining flour, cocoa powder, baking powder and salt. Add the sugar, beaten eggs, olive oil, Tabasco/hot pepper sauce, vanilla, melted chocolate and 250 ml/1 cup water, and mix until thoroughly blended.

Pour into the prepared cake pan and bake on the middle shelf of the preheated oven for 45 minutes, until the top is no longer shiny and has formed a light crust – the inside will still be slightly soft.

Let the cake cool for at least 15 minutes before removing from the pan and transferring to a wire cooling rack. Leave the oven on.

Prepare the ganache – tip the chopped chocolate into a bowl. Heat the cream, butter, brown sugar and a few drops of Tabasco/hot pepper sauce in a small pan until boiling, stir until smooth, then pour over the chopped chocolate. Leave for 2 minutes, stir until smooth and leave to cool and thicken slightly.

Meanwhile, make the garnish. Thinly slice the chilli/chile and roll in the sugar. Place the chilli/chile slices on the lined baking sheet and bake in the oven for 5–10 minutes or until the sugar begins to crystallize. Once this has happened, place the chilli/chile slices back in the sugar to add even more crunch.

Place the cooled cake on a serving plate and coat the top and sides with the ganache. Decorate with the candied chillies/chiles.

Chai macarons

Gently spiced chai tea, originally from Nepal, is one of my favourite drinks and I love pairing it with chocolate. The Aztecs discovered chocolate and used it to make a drink made with spices, making this a perfect little nod to how chocolate would have originally been consumed.

Chocolate macarons
175 g/1¾ cups ground almonds
175 g/1¼ cups icing/ confectioners' sugar
5 egg whites
200 g/1 cup caster/ granulated sugar
1 teaspoon pure vanilla extract
20 g/2 tablespoons cocoa powder, sifted

Chai ganache
85 ml/⅓ cup whole milk
1 Earl Grey tea bag
1 cinnamon stick
1 whole clove
2 black peppercorns
2–3 cardamom pods
1 star anise
a large pinch of freshly grated nutmeg
a pinch of salt
200 g/1½ cups milk/ semisweet chocolate, finely chopped

2 large baking sheets
baking parchment
a 4-cm/1½-inch round cookie cutter
2 piping/pastry bag fitted with plain nozzles/tips

Makes 30

Take two sheets of baking parchment and, using the cookie cutter as a guide, draw 30 circles on each sheet, spacing them evenly. Place upside-down on baking sheets, so that the lines are on the underside (you should be able to see them through the paper).

Combine the ground almonds and icing/ confectioners' sugar in a food processor, and blitz for 30–60 seconds to finely grind. Tip into a bowl, add 50 g/2 oz. of the egg whites and beat until combined into a paste. Set aside.

Fill a saucepan or pot with water to a depth of 10 cm/4 inches, and bring to a gentle simmer.

Tip the remaining egg whites into a heatproof bowl and set over the prepared pan/pot of simmering water. Add the caster/granulated sugar. Using a handheld electric whisk, slowly beat the egg whites and sugar until combined. Continue to whisk for about 3 minutes, until the sugar has dissolved and the mixture is thick, glossy, white and warm to the touch.

Remove the bowl from the pan and continue to whisk on medium-fast speed for another 3 minutes until cool and very thick. Add the vanilla extract and sifted cocoa powder, and fold in using a large metal spoon.

Take a quarter of the meringue and add to the ground almond mixture, stirring to combine and loosen the mixture. Add this back to the meringue and fold in, in large strokes. Continue to mix until thoroughly combined and the mixture holds a ribbon trail for about 5 seconds.

Working quickly, scoop the mixture into one of the prepared piping/pastry bags and pipe 30 macarons onto each baking sheet, using the circles as a guide. Set aside for 30 minutes, until a light skin has formed on the surface.

Preheat the oven to 160°C (325°F) Gas 3.

Bake the macarons, one sheet at a time, on the middle shelf of the oven for 10–12 minutes, until well risen and crisp on top. Leave to cool completely on the baking sheets.

To make the ganache, put the milk in a small saucepan with the tea bag and the spices. Bring to just below boiling and remove from the heat immediately. Leave to infuse for 1 hour.

Tip the chopped chocolate into a heatproof bowl. Bring the spiced chai milk back to the boil and strain into the bowl over the chopped chocolate. Stir gently to combine and to allow the chocolate to melt smoothly into the hot milk. Leave to cool and thicken slightly.

Fill the other prepared piping/pastry bag with the ganache. Pipe a circle on the flat-side of half of the macarons and sandwich with a second. Leave for 30 minutes before serving.

Billionaire's shortbread

Shortbread base
**150 g/1 stick plus
2 tablespoons unsalted
butter, softened**
**125 g/scant ⅔ cup caster/
granulated sugar**
3 egg yolks
**200 g/1⅔ cups plain/
all-purpose flour**
**⅛ teaspoon baking
powder**
a pinch of salt

Chocolate salted caramel
**200 g/1 cup caster/
granulated sugar**
**200 ml/¾ cup double/
heavy cream**
**2 tablespoons golden/
light corn syrup**
**1 teaspoon pure vanilla
extract**
**a large pinch of sea salt
flakes**
**50 g/3½ tablespoons
unsalted butter**
**50 g/⅓ cup dark/
bittersweet chocolate
(70%), finely chopped**
**50 g/⅓ cup milk/
semisweet chocolate,
finely chopped**

To finish
**250 g/2 cups dark/
bittersweet chocolate
edible gold spray**

*20 x 30-cm/8 x 12-inch
baking pan, greased
and lined with baking
parchment*
a sugar thermometer

Makes 16–20

I am a self-confessed lover of millionaire's shortbread but I wanted to give it a face lift by making it totally chocolate-based, giving it the billionaire treatment. The chocolate aerated shortbread is topped with a rich chocolate caramel and finished with crunchy chocolate and gold lustre. I don't know many billionaires but I bet they'd love this!

Cream the butter and sugar together until pale and light using a handheld electric whisk. Add the egg yolks, one at time, mixing well between each addition.

Sift the flour, baking powder and salt into the bowl and mix again until thoroughly combined. Bring the dough together into a smooth ball, flatten into a rectangular slab and roll out into a neat 20 x 30-cm/8 x 12-inch rectangle between two pieces of lightly floured baking parchment. Use the baking pan as a guide to the required size. Peel off the top sheet of paper and flip the pastry over into the lined pan, press the pastry smooth, peel off the top parchment and chill for 20 minutes while you preheat the oven to 170°C (325°F) Gas 3.

Bake the shortbread base on the middle shelf of the preheated oven for about 15 minutes, until golden. Remove from the oven and to cool completely.

To make the chocolate salted caramel put the sugar into a medium pan, add 1–2 tablespoons of water and heat gently to dissolve the sugar without stirring. Increase the heat and continue to cook the syrup until it becomes an amber-coloured caramel. Remove from the heat and slowly add the cream with the golden/light corn syrup and vanilla.

Return to the heat, put the sugar thermometer into the pan and bring slowly back to the boil to melt any hardened caramel. Simmer gently for about 4 minutes until the sauce has thickened and the caramel has reached a temperature of 110°C (225°F). Simmer at this heat for 1 minute. If you don't have a thermometer drop half a teaspoon of the caramel into a bowl of ice cold water, and it should firm into a very soft ball.

Remove from the heat, add the salt and butter, stir until combined and then leave to cool for at least 5–10 minutes before adding the chopped dark/bittersweet and milk/semisweet chocolates. If you add the chocolate sooner, you risk the mixture splitting. Mix until the chocolate has completely melted into the caramel and then pour onto the shortbread base in a smooth, even layer. Leave for at least 2 hours, until completely cold and set.

Melt the remaining 250 g/2 cups dark/bittersweet chocolate over a bain marie, stirring until smooth. Remove from the heat, cool slightly then pour evenly over the caramel base and leave to set firm before spraying with edible gold spray.

Using a hot knife, cut the shortbread into squares to serve.

Chocolate brioche doughnuts

A trip to the penny arcade on a British seaside pier, full of flashing lights, the sounds of coins being dropped into slot machines and of laughter with a bag full of hot, sugar-encrusted doughnuts in my hand is my idea of a good time! I've given the humble doughnut a new lease of life here by basing the dough on brioche so it's made with lots more butter and has the addition of cocoa powder and chocolate. The chocolate dipping sauce takes these sugary treats to a whole new level of delicious!

200 ml/¾ cup whole milk

1 x 11-g/⅓-oz. active dried yeast

1 teaspoon clear honey

425 g/3⅓ cups strong white bread flour, plus extra for dusting

40 g/⅓ cup cocoa powder

75 g/generous ⅓ cup caster/superfine sugar

½ teaspoon salt

1 egg, beaten

2 egg yolks

75 g/5 tablespoons unsalted butter, softened

50 g/⅓ cup dark/bittersweet chocolate, coarsely grated

1½–2 litres/6–8 cups sunflower or groundnut oil, for deep frying

200 g/1 cup caster/superfine sugar

chocolate sauce, to serve (see page 124)

a 6-cm/2½-inch round cookie cutter

a sugar thermometer

Makes about 20–24 small doughnuts

Heat the milk until warm but not too hot, add the yeast and honey or maple syrup, whisk to dissolve the yeast and leave in a warm place for 5 minutes to activate the yeast and for it to have formed a thick foam on top of the milk.

Tip the flour, cocoa, sugar and salt into the bowl of a stand mixer fitted with a dough hook. Make a well in the centre of the dry ingredients, add the yeasty milk, whole egg, egg yolks and unsalted butter. Mix steadily for about 5 minutes until the dough is smooth and elastic. It will still be slightly sticky. Add the grated chocolate and mix again until incorporated.

Very lightly dust the work surface with a little flour, scrape the dough out of the mixing bowl and knead again using your hands for 30 seconds. Shape the dough in to a smooth ball and place in a large, lightly oiled mixing bowl. Cover with clingfilm/plastic wrap and leave to prove in a warm place for 2 hours, or until the dough has doubled in size.

Lightly dust the work surface with flour again and knead the dough very gently for 1 minute. Roll the dough out to a thickness of just over 1 cm/½ inch.

Using the round cookie cutter, stamp out discs from the dough and arrange on the prepared baking trays, leaving space between each doughnut. Gather any scraps together, knead to combine and re-roll and stamp out more doughnuts. Loosely cover the trays with clingfilm/plastic wrap and leave to rise again for 30–40 minutes.

Pour the sunflower oil into a large, shallow saucepan; it should come at least half way up the sides of the pan. Put a thermometer into the oil and heat to 180°C (350°F). Cover a large baking sheet with a triple thickness of paper towels and tip the caster/superfine sugar for dusting into a large bowl.

Fry the doughnuts, in batches of 4 or 5, for 2 minutes on each side, or until nearly doubled in size and lightly browned all over. Remove with a slotted spoon and drain thoroughly on the paper towels before tossing the warm doughnuts in the sugar. Make sure that the oil comes back up to temperature before frying the next batch of doughnuts.

Best eaten on the day of making and serving with a bowl of ganache or chocolate sauce for dunking.

Desserts & puddings

Chocolate, honey & raspberry tart

This is one of my dinner party favourites – a simple chocolate and honey tart, topped with beautiful fresh raspberries. I love the chocolate pastry filled with rich chocolate ganache. You can of course make the tart using honey, as here, but if you can get your hands on honey-flavoured chocolate made with honey powder, use it – the underlying honey flavour that comes through is a treat!

Pâte sablée
**200 g/1 stick plus
  5 tablespoons unsalted
  butter, softened**
**100 g/¾ cup icing/
  confectioners' sugar,
  plus extra for dusting**
a pinch of salt
1 vanilla pod/bean
**finely grated zest of
  ½ orange**
2 eggs, lightly beaten
**200 g/1⅔ cups plain/
  all-purpose flour, plus
  extra for rolling out**
50 g/⅓ cup cocoa powder

Ganache
**350 g/3 cups dark/
  bittersweet chocolate,
  chopped**
**75 g/½ cup milk/
  semisweet chocolate,
  chopped**
**300 ml/1¼ cups
  whipping/heavy cream**
**50 g/3½ tablespoons
  unsalted butter**
**1 tablespoon liquid
  glucose**
**2 tablespoons clear
  orange blossom honey**
a pinch of salt
400 g/4 cups raspberries

*a 23-cm/9-inch fluted
  tart pan*
baking beans

Serves 8–10

Begin by making the *pâte sablée*. Put the butter, icing/confectioners' sugar and salt in a large mixing bowl and cream together with an electric whisk for about 5 minutes, or until a pale cream colour.

Split the vanilla pod/bean lengthwise using a small, sharp knife and scrape the seeds out into the creamed butter mixture, discarding the shell. Add the orange zest and mix.

Gradually add the eggs, whisking all the time, until fully incorporated. Gently mix in the flour and cocoa powder, taking care not to overwork the dough. Bring the dough together and form a ball with your hands. Wrap in clingfilm/plastic wrap, flatten into a disc and chill for at least 2 hours or until needed.

Roll out the dough to a thickness of about 2 mm/⅛ inch on a lightly floured surface. Neatly line the tart pan with the pastry and trim off any excess from around the edges with a small, sharp knife. Prick the base with a fork and chill in the fridge for 20 minutes.

Preheat the oven to 180°C (350°F) Gas 4.

Line the pastry case with baking parchment, fill with baking beans and bake blind on a baking sheet on the middle shelf of the oven for about 20 minutes, or until pale golden. Remove from the oven and discard the parchment and beans. Return the case to the oven and continue to cook for a further 5 minutes, or until crisp. Remove from the oven and set aside to cool.

To make the ganache, tip the chopped chocolates into a medium-sized bowl and set aside. Put the cream, butter, glucose, honey and a pinch of salt in a saucepan or pot set over a medium heat and bring to the boil. Pour the hot cream mixture over the chocolate and stir until melted, smooth and silky. Pour the ganache into the baked pastry case and chill in the fridge until firm.

Arrange the raspberries on the top of the tart, dust with icing/confectioners' sugar and cut into slices to serve.

A **B**

Feuilletine base

**90 g/⅔ cup milk/
   semisweet chocolate,
   chopped**

**25 g/2 tablespoons
   unsalted butter**

**50 g/¼ tablespoon
   hazelnut paste**

90 g/1 cup feuilletine

Chocolate sponge

2 egg whites

**50 g/¼ cup caster/
   granulated sugar**

2 eggs

**75 g/¾ cup ground
   almonds**

**50 g/⅓ cup icing/
   confectioners' sugar**

**10 g/2 teaspoons plain/
   all-purpose flour**

**10 g/2 teaspoons cocoa
   powder**

**15 g/1 tablespoon
   unsalted butter, melted**

Jelly/jello

**300 g/1½ cups canned
   apricots**

**4 leaves platinum-grade
   gelatine**

**½ vanilla pod/bean,
   cut in half lengthways**

**200 ml/¾ cup freshly
   squeezed orange juice**

**40 g/¼ cup caster/
   granulated sugar**

continued overleaf

Apricot & rosemary délice

This dessert is based on the flavours of the famous sachertorte from Austria but given the Will treatment in the form of a chocolate mousse infused with rosemary atop crunchy feuilletine – brittle, crispy praline flakes. The addition of rosemary in the chocolate mousse gives a savoury note to this dessert without being overpowering, allowing the apricot to shine through in flavour and colour.

Start by making the feuilletine base. Melt the chocolate and butter in a heatproof bowl set over a saucepan or pot of barely simmering water, or in the microwave on a low setting. Stir until smooth and set aside to cool slightly. Add the hazelnut paste and feuilletine and mix until thoroughly combined. Scoop the mixture into the prepared baking pan and press into a thin, even layer, covering the base, using the back of a spoon. Pop in the fridge to chill and firm up while you prepare the cake layer. **(A, B)**

Preheat the oven to 190°C (375°F) Gas 5.

Whisk the egg whites and caster/granulated sugar together in a large mixing bowl until they hold stiff peaks – this is more easily achieved using a stand mixer or an electric hand whisk. Add the whole eggs and whisk briefly to combine. Sift in the ground almonds, icing/confectioners' sugar, plain/all-purpose flour and cocoa powder, and using a large metal spoon fold the ingredients together. Gently fold in the melted butter.

Remove the feuilletine base from the fridge and spoon over the cake batter. Gently spread the batter level using an off-set palette knife. Cook on the middle shelf of the preheated oven for 8–10 minutes, or until springy to the touch.

To make the jelly, whizz 200 g/1 cup of the apricots until smooth using a food processor

Rosemary mousse

**60 g/⅓ cup caster/
superfine sugar**

**400 ml/1⅔ cups double/
heavy cream, whipped**

2 sprigs rosemary

**125 g/1 cup dark/
bittersweet chocolate
(70%), finely chopped**

Chocolate glaze

**100 g/3½ oz./¾ cup dark/
bittersweet chocolate
(70%)**

**45 g/3¼ tablespoons
unsalted butter**

**40 g/scant ¼ cup whole
milk**

**15 g/1 tablespoon clear
honey**

*a 30 x 15-cm/12 x 6-inch
baking pan, greased
and lined with baking
parchment (let run over
the outside edges)*

Serves 16

and dice the remaining 100 g/½ cup into
1-cm/⅜-inch cubes, mix together in a bowl
and set aside. In a separate bowl, soak the
gelatine leaves in cold water for 10 minutes
to soften. Meanwhile, put the split vanilla
pod/bean into a small saucepan/pot with the
orange juice and caster/granulated sugar set
over a medium heat. Bring to the boil, stirring
to dissolve the sugar. Remove the pan from
the heat, then drain the gelatine, blot briefly
on a paper towel to remove any excess water
and add it to the hot juice mixture. Whisk to
combine and strain over the reserved apricot
purée and cubes. Stir to combine and plunge
the bowl into a sink of ice-cold water to speed
up the cooling process. Once the jelly starts
to set and thicken, pour over the sponge and
leave to set firm in the fridge – about 2 hours.

To make the mousse, place the caster/superfine
sugar into a saucepan or pot set over a low
heat and cook until it begins to caramelize.
In a separate saucepan or pot, heat 125 ml/
½ cup of the cream with the rosemary and
slowly bring to the boil. **(C)** Meanwhile, whip
the remaining cream to soft peaks and set
aside. When the sugar has turned a golden

amber colour, gradually strain the hot cream
into the pan, being very careful as it will
splutter, stirring constantly with a long
handled wooden spoon or spatula until
smooth. The sugar will bubble up but there
is no need to panic that's just what it does!
Once all the hot cream has been added, pour
the caramel cream over the chopped
chocolate and mix thoroughly. **(D)** Set aside
to cool for 3–5 minutes and then fold through
the whipped cream to create a mousse. **(E)**

Spoon the mousse onto the set jelly and
spread level with an off-set palette knife.
Put in the freezer to set for no more than
an hour or in the fridge for at least 4 hours.

To make the chocolate glaze, combine all
of the ingredients in a small saucepan or pot
set over a low–medium heat and cook until
smooth and shiny. Cool slightly, then pour
the glaze over the top of the mousse in an
even layer. Chill in the fridge for at least
30 minutes before serving.

Lift the délice from the pan using the baking
parchment. With a hot knife, cut into
5 x 15-cm/2 x 6-inch rectangles and serve.

Chocolate & hazelnut 'melt-in-the-middle' pudding

When I go out for dinner, if there is a chocolate fondant on the menu, I always order it. The soft, almost fudgy, sponge encases liquid chocolate in a way that is just perfect! I had one of the best chocolate fondants ever when I cooked with Michelin-starred chef John Campbell, who cooked his in the microwave – trust me when I say they were heavenly! My melt-in-the-middles are made with hazelnuts, Frangelico – an Italian hazelnut liqueur – and a ganache centre that oozes beautifully when you cut in with a spoon.

225 g/2 sticks unsalted butter
225 g/1²⁄₃ cups dark/bittersweet chocolate, chopped
4 eggs
2 egg yolks
175 g/³⁄₄ cup plus 2 tablespoons caster/granulated sugar
1 teaspoon pure vanilla extract
a pinch of salt
10 g/2 teaspoons cocoa powder
40 g/¹⁄₃ cup plain/all-purpose flour
40 g/¹⁄₃ cup ground hazelnuts
8 teaspoons ganache (see pages 30–31)

8 x 175-ml/6-oz. capacity ramekins, greased and dusted with cocoa powder

Makes 8

Preheat the oven to 190°C (375°F) Gas 5.

Melt the butter and chopped chocolate in a heatproof bowl set over a saucepan or pot of simmering water. Stir until smooth, then remove from the heat and set aside to cool.

In a separate bowl, whisk together the eggs, egg yolks, sugar, vanilla and salt for about 3 minutes, until it has at least doubled in volume, pale and mousse-like – this is more easily achieved using a stand mixer or an electric hand whisk.

Using a rubber spatula or large metal spoon, fold the melted chocolate and butter into the egg mixture, being careful not to knock out too much air. Sift in the cocoa powder, flour and ground hazelnuts and gently fold to combine.

Half fill each of the prepared ramekins with the fondant mixture and place a teaspoon of hazelnut ganache in the middle of the fondant mixture. Divide the remaining fondant mixture between the ramekins, filling each one almost to the top but leaving a gap of about ½ cm/¼ inch.

Arrange the ramekins on a large baking sheet and cook on the middle shelf of the preheated oven for 10–12 minutes. The fondants should be well-risen and still soft in the middle.

Remove from the oven and set aside to rest in the ramekins for 30 seconds–1 minute, then run a palette knife around the edges to turn the fondants out onto plates. Serve immediately and watch the middle melt.

Salted caramel honeycomb & chocolate profiteroles

Choux/cream puff pastry
125 ml/½ cup milk
100 g/7 tablespoons unsalted butter, diced
a pinch of salt
a pinch of caster/ granulated sugar
140 g/generous 1 cup plain/all-purpose flour, sifted
5–6 medium eggs

Filling
500 ml/2 cups milk
the seeds of 1 vanilla pod/bean
50 g/¼ cup caster/ granulated sugar
200 g/⅔ cup ready-made canned caramel, such as Carnation
4 large egg yolks
3 tablespoons cornflour/ cornstarch
25 g/2 tablespoons unsalted butter
a pinch of sea salt flakes
300 ml/1¼ cups double/ heavy cream
75 g/⅓ cup crushed honeycomb pieces

Chocolate sauce
50 g/¼ cup caster/ granulated sugar
300 ml/1¼ cups double/ heavy cream
150 g/1¼ cup dark/ bittersweet chocolate, chopped

2 piping/pastry bags fitted with a plain nozzle/tip
2 baking sheets, greased and lined with baking parchment

Makes about 32 buns/ puffs and serves 6–8

Profiteroles are, for me, the ultimate dessert for a party. A leaning tower of profiteroles stacked up, with a drizzle of hot chocolate sauce and filled with a salted caramel crème diplomate and crushed honeycomb is delicious.

Preheat the oven to 180°C (350°F) Gas 4.

To make the choux/cream puff pastry, put 125 ml/½ cup of water, the milk, butter, salt and sugar into a medium saucepan or pot set over a medium heat. Stir constantly to melt the butter. As soon as the mixture comes to the boil, reduce the heat and, working very quickly, shoot in the flour. Beat vigorously over the heat for 3 minutes, until the mixture is smooth and cleanly leaves the sides of the pan.

Transfer the dough to a large mixing bowl and, using an electric whisk, beat in the eggs one at a time. You might not need all of the eggs – the dough is ready when it is soft and smooth and drops off a spoon leaving a 'V' shape behind.

Scoop the dough into one of the prepared piping/pastry bags and pipe 16 buns onto each prepared baking sheet leaving plenty of space between each one. Bake on the middle shelves of the preheated oven for 10–15 minutes until well-risen, golden brown and hollow in the middle. Transfer to a wire rack to cool.

To make the filling, heat the milk with the vanilla seeds until just boiling. In a mixing bowl, whisk together the sugar, caramel, egg yolks and cornflour/cornstarch until smooth and creamy. Whisking constantly, pour half of the hot milk into the bowl and continue to whisk until smooth. Pour the contents of the bowl back into the pan and whisk over a low heat until the sauce starts to bubble and thicken. Continue to cook for 2–3 minutes.

Remove from the heat, add the butter, a large pinch of sea salt flakes and the honeycomb pieces, and mix until glossy. Pour the mixture into a clean bowl and cover the surface with clingfilm/plastic wrap to prevent a skin forming. Set aside to cool then chill for about 4 hours.

To make the chocolate sauce, tip the sugar into a small saucepan or pot set over a low heat. Add ½ tablespoon of water, and dissolve the sugar without stirring. Bring to the boil and continue to cook the syrup until it becomes an amber-colored caramel. Remove the pan from the heat and slowly add the cream, stirring constantly to combine. Return the pan to a low heat to melt any hardened caramel that might have formed on the bottom of the pan. Once the caramel cream is smooth but not quite boiling, add the chocolate, remove from the heat and stir gently until thoroughly combined. Let cool to room temperature.

Whip the cream until it holds soft, billowing peaks and then fold in the chilled caramel mixture using a large metal spoon. Stir through the crushed honeycomb. Scoop into the other piping/pastry bag, then, using a metal skewer, make a hole on the underside of each bun and pipe in the filling.

Arrange the profiteroles on a large serving plate and pour chocolate sauce over the top.

Steamed chocolate pudding & custard

When I was at school, I used to love school dinners. I was probably one of only a few. One dish I remember fondly was a steamed chocolate sponge pudding with chocolate custard. Large trays of the steamed sponge with thick and gloopy custard would appear and I loved it! This is my homage to school dinners, albeit with a poshed-up chocolate custard sauce in place of the thick, lumpy stuff.

175 g/1½ sticks unsalted butter, softened, plus extra for greasing
100 g/½ cup soft light brown sugar
75 g/½ cup caster/granulated sugar
3 large eggs
1 teaspoon pure vanilla extract
150 g/1 cup plus 2 tablespoons self-raising/rising flour
50 g/⅓ cup cocoa powder
a pinch of salt
3 tablespoons milk

Custard sauce
600 ml/2⅓ cups whole milk
1 vanilla pod/bean, split
5 large egg yolks
100 g/½ cup caster/granulated sugar
1 tablespoon cocoa powder
50 g/⅓ cup dark/bittersweet chocolate, finely chopped

a 1¼-litre/40-oz. pudding basin, greased

Serves 6

In the bowl of a stand mixer, cream the butter together with both sugars until pale and light, scraping down the sides of the bowl with a rubber spatula from time to time. Gradually add the eggs, mixing well between each addition. Add the vanilla and mix again.

Sift the flour, cocoa powder and salt into the bowl, add the milk and mix until smooth. Spoon the batter into the prepared pudding basin and spread level. Cover the top of the pudding with pleated sheets of buttered baking parchment and then foil – this allows room for the pudding to rise as it cooks. Tie the foil and paper securely under the lip/rim of the pudding basin and trim off any excess paper leaving a frill of 2 cm/¾ inch. Fold this frill back on itself so that it sits on top of the covered pudding and won't hang in the pan water.

Bring a large saucepan or pot of water to a simmer over a medium heat and lower the pudding into it. The water should come halfway up the side of the basin. Cover with a lid and steam for 1½–1¾ hours, until cooked through and well risen. You may need to top up the water after an hour.

Remove the steamed pudding from the pan and set aside to cool slightly.

To make the custard sauce, pour the milk into a saucepan or pot set over a medium heat. Add the split vanilla pod/bean, then bring the mixture slowly to the boil. Remove the pan from the heat and set aside for about 20 minutes for the vanilla to fully infuse the milk.

In a separate bowl, beat the egg yolks, sugar and cocoa powder together until pale and creamy. Reheat the milk and pour onto the egg mixture, whisking constantly until smooth. Pour the custard back into the pan and put over a low heat. Stirring constantly, cook until the custard is thick enough to coat the back of a spoon. Add the chopped chocolate and whisk until melted and thoroughly combined.

Remove the baking parchment and foil lid from the steamed pudding, place a serving plate over the top and turn out.

Strain the custard into a jug/pitcher and serve poured over the top of the hot pudding.

Chocolate & chestnut roulade

Roulade
4 large eggs
150 g/¾ cup caster/
  granulated sugar, plus
  extra for rolling
1 teaspoon pure vanilla
  extract
100 g/¾ cup plain/
  all-purpose flour
25 g/⅓ cup cocoa powder
½ teaspoon baking
  powder
a pinch of salt
50 g/3½ tablespoons
  unsalted butter, melted

Buttercream
200 g/1½ cups dark/
  bittersweet chocolate,
  chopped
3 large egg whites
200 g/1 cup caster/
  granulated sugar
a pinch of salt
250 g/2 sticks plus
  1 tablespoon unsalted
  butter, softened and
  diced
1 x 250-g/8½-oz. can
  sweetened chestnut
  purée/spread
marron glacé, chopped

To serve
chocolate shavings
cocoa powder, for dusting

*a 40 x 30-cm/16 x 12-inch
swiss/jelly roll pan, greased
and lined with baking
parchment*

Serves 6–8

We always have a chocolate yule log at Christmas, it's just a family tradition. I've added chestnut purée to a chocolate buttercream to roll my soft chocolate sponge with instead of traditional whipped cream and decorated it with chopped chocolate. It's rustic, easy to prepare and perfect for Christmas day!

Preheat the oven to 180°C (350°F) Gas 4.

To make the roulade, put the eggs, sugar and vanilla into a large mixing bowl and whisk with a handheld electric whisk for about 5 minutes, until the mixture is pale and thick and has trebled in volume.

Sift the flour, cocoa powder, baking powder and salt into the bowl and gently fold into the egg mixture using a large metal spoon, taking care not to knock out too much air. Carefully pour the cooled, melted butter around the edge of the bowl and fold in until there are no traces of it.

Spoon or pour the batter into the prepared pan and gently spread level with a palette knife. Bake on the middle shelf of the preheated oven for 8–10 minutes, or until well-risen with a light crust and the cake springs back when lightly pressed with your finger. Let the cake cool in the pan for a minute.

Meanwhile, lay a large sheet of baking parchment on a clean work surface and scatter with 1 tablespoon caster/granulated sugar. Carefully turn the roulade out of the pan onto the sugar-coated paper and peel off the paper lining. Lay a clean dish towel on top of the cake and, starting at one of the shorter edges, roll the cake into a tight spiral with the towel inside the roll. Set aside until completely cold.

To make the buttercream, melt the chocolate in a heatproof bowl set over a saucepan or pot

of barely simmering water. Stir until smooth and set aside.

To make the meringue, put the egg whites, sugar and salt in a separate heatproof bowl set over a saucepan or pot of simmering water. Add 2 tablespoons of water and whisk until the sugar has completely dissolved and the mixture is foamy. Continue to cook for about 5 minutes, until the mixture is warm to the touch, thickens, turns bright white and will hold a ribbon trail.

Pour the mixture into a large mixing bowl and beat for about 3 minutes with an electric handheld whisk, until it has doubled in volume is thick, stiff, glossy and the outside of the bowl feels cold to the touch.

Gradually add the butter to the cold meringue mixture, beating constantly on low–medium speed, until the frosting is smooth. Using a large spoon or spatula fold in the melted chocolate and the chestnut purée/spread.

To assemble the roulade, carefully unroll the cooled cake and remove the dish towel. Spoon 4 generous tablespoons of buttercream onto the cake and spread evenly using a palette knife. Scatter with the chopped marron glacé. Using the baking parchment to support the cake, roll the cake back into a tight spiral and transfer to a serving plate. Cover the whole cake with more buttercream, scatter with chocolate shavings and dust with cocoa powder to serve.

White chocolate cheesecake with strawberries & basil

This baked cheesecake is made with white chocolate and cream cheese for a lovely open yet creamy texture. The base is made with biscotti cookies which give a great crunchy texture but also a delicious flavour. Topped with a strawberry salad tumbled with baby basil and olive oil that cuts through the richness of the cheesecake, it is a wonderful dessert for a summer party.

175 g/6 oz. plain biscotti

75 g/5 tablespoons unsalted butter, melted

175 g/1⅓ cups white chocolate, chopped

600 g/3 cups full-fat cream cheese

3 large eggs

300 ml/1¼ cups soured cream

175 g/¾ cup caster/ granulated sugar

1 tablespoon cornflour/ cornstarch

1 teaspoon pure vanilla extract

freshly squeezed juice and grated zest of 1 lemon

To serve

250 g/2½ cups strawberries, hulled and quartered

1 small bunch baby basil

4–5 tablespoons fruity extra virgin olive oil

a 20-cm/8-inch round springform cake pan, greased and lined with baking parchment

Serves 8–10

Preheat the oven to 170°C (300°F) Gas 3.

Crush the biscotti in a freezer bag using a rolling pin and tip into a large mixing bowl. Pour the melted butter into the crumbs and stir to combine. Tip the mixture into the prepared pan and press into an even layer with the back of a metal spoon to form a base. Bake on the middle shelf of the preheated oven for 5 minutes. Remove and set aside to cool. Do not turn the oven off.

Melt the chocolate in a heatproof bowl set over a saucepan or pot of barely simmering water. Stir until smooth and glossy and remove from the heat.

Put the cream cheese, eggs, soured cream, sugar and cornflour/cornstarch into a food processor and whizz until smooth. Scrape down the sides of the bowl with a rubber spatula, then add the vanilla, lemon juice and zest and whizz again.

Carefully pour the mixture into the pan on top of the baked biscotti base. Place on a baking sheet and bake on the middle shelf of the still-warm oven for 40 minutes, or until just set.

Remove the cheesecake from the oven and let it cool completely before chilling in the fridge.

To serve, mix the hulled and quartered strawberries together with the baby basil leaves and extra virgin olive oil. Heap the drowned strawberries on top of the chilled cheesecake and serve in slices.

Mississippi banoffee mud pies

I love to combine different flavours and desserts into one! So here I've taken two of my favourite big and bold American desserts; Mississippi mud pies and banoffee pie, and mashed them into one. Adding a layer of caramel mixed with caramelized banana purée gives a lovely texture and flavour to the classic chocolate and cream combo of Mississippi mud pies. If you want to, you can add a the zest and juice of a lime to the caramel to work in another famous American dessert; key lime pie. It's pie, thrice!

Base
300 g/10 oz. chocolate coated digestive biscuits/graham crackers
75 g/5 tablespoons unsalted butter, melted

Caramel banana sauce
15 g/1 tablespoon unsalted butter
3 large ripe bananas, sliced
75 g/generous ⅓ cup caster/granulated sugar
400 g/1¾ cups canned ready-made caramel, such as Carnation

Chocolate mousse
2 leaves gelatine
125 g/½ cup plus 2 tablespoons caster/superfine sugar
800 ml/3¼ cups whipping/heavy cream
200 g/1½ cups dark/bittersweet chocolate, chopped
a pinch of salt

To finish
400 ml/1⅔ cups double/heavy cream
chocolate shavings

8 x 9-cm/3½-inch round fluted tartlet pans with removable bases

Serves 8

Break the digestive biscuits/graham crackers into pieces and put into a food processor. Whizz until finely chopped and transfer to a large mixing bowl. Pour in the melted butter and cocoa powder and stir well to combine. Press the buttery crumbs into the prepared tartlet pans in an even layer to cover the base and sides. Cover and chill in the fridge for 20 minutes while you prepare the caramelized banana layer.

To make the caramel banana sauce, heat the butter in a large frying pan/skillet set over a medium heat. Add the sliced bananas and cook until they start to soften. Add the sugar and continue to cook until the bananas have caramelized and are coated in amber-coloured caramel. Transfer to a food processor and blend until smooth. Tip into a bowl, add the caramel and mix until thoroughly combined.

To make the mousse; soak the gelatine leaves in cold water for 10 minutes to soften. Meanwhile, tip the sugar into a small, heavy-bottomed saucepan or pot set over a low–medium heat. Add 1 tablespoon of water and dissolve the sugar without stirring. Bring to the boil and continue to cook until the sugar becomes an amber-coloured caramel. Swirl the pan if necessary to ensure the caramel cooks evenly.

In another saucepan or pot, bring 240 ml/scant 1 cup of the cream to the boil. Slowly and carefully pour the hot cream into the caramel in stages, it will bubble furiously at first. Stir until smooth and remove from the heat.

Tip the chopped chocolate into a heatproof bowl. Drain the gelatine, blot briefly on a paper towel to remove any excess water. Pour the caramel cream into the chocolate, add the gelatine and mix until smooth. Set aside to cool.

In another bowl whip the remaining cream until it holds soft peaks. Fold the whipped cream into the chocolate cream mixture.

Divide the caramel banana sauce evenly between the chilled tartlet cases. Top with the chocolate mousse, filling each pie to the top and spreading smooth with a palette knife. Chill in the fridge until firm.

To finish, whip the cream until it holds floppy peaks. Spoon on top of the pies, scatter with chocolate shavings and serve immediately.

Chocolate, pear and ginger crumble

This is a really warming winter dessert that is perfect for chocolate lovers. I made this first when I had some leftover ingredients; chocolate-coated ginger cookies, chocolate truffles and some pears poached in red wine. I just put them all together and this dessert was born. The truffles melt beautifully into the pears and red wine mixture creating an almost mulled wine chocolate sauce. With the crunchy crumbs on top it was a pretty good dessert as it was, but here it is with little extra flair thrown in for good measure.

Red wine ganache
125 g/1 cup dark/bittersweet chocolate, finely chopped
90 ml/⅓ cup red wine

Pear filling
6 pears, peeled and cored and chopped
75 ml/scant ⅓ cup red wine
25 ml/2 tablespoons ruby port
75 g/¼ cup clear honey
1 star anise
1 cinnamon stick
150 g/1½ cups blackberries or blackcurrants

Crumble
110 g/¾ cup blanched hazelnuts
75 g/generous ½ cup plain/all-purpose flour
1 tablespoon cocoa powder
50 g/¼ cup soft light brown sugar
75 g/5 tablespoons unsalted butter, chilled and diced
1 teaspoon ground cinnamon
1 teaspoon mixed/apple pie spice
a pinch of salt

a 23-cm/9-inch ovenproof baking dish

Serves 8

Begin by preparing the ganache. Put the chopped chocolate into a heatproof bowl and set aside. Heat the red wine in a small saucepan or pot set over a medium heat to just below boiling. Pour over the chocolate and stir until smooth. Let cool, cover and chill in the fridge until firm.

For the pear filling, put the chopped pears in a saucepan or pot with the red wine, port and honey. Add the star anise and cinnamon stick, set the pan over a medium heat and cook for about 10 minutes, until the pears start to soften. Add the blackberries, stir and transfer to the ovenproof dish. Set aside to cool.

Preheat the oven to 180°C (350°F) Gas 4.

To make the crumble, tip 40 g/¼ cup of the blanched hazelnuts into a food processor and blitz to a roughly chopped consistency. Transfer to a large mixing bowl and set aside.

Tip the remaining hazelnuts into the food processor and whizz until finely ground. Add the flour, cocoa powder, sugar, diced butter, spices and salt and whizz again until the butter has been rubbed into the dry ingredients and the mixture starts to clump together. Transfer to the bowl with the chopped hazelnuts and mix. Pour the crumble mixture onto a baking sheet in an even layer and bake on the middle shelf of the preheated oven for 20 minutes, or until it starts to crisp.

To assemble the crumble, scoop teaspoons of the red wine ganache around the pears and blackberries in the baking dish. Top with the pre-baked crumble and bake in the oven for 20 minutes until the fruit is bubbling and the topping is crisp.

Remove from the oven and serve immediately.

Chocolate cranachan 'pavlova-dose'

Pavlova is one of those desserts that just looks so inviting when the fruit and cream appear to have been simply thrown on and the voluptuous whipped cream and fruit are tumbled on top – it is a perfect summer dessert. My Scottish heritage means I love a good cranachan, a heady mix of toasted oats, smoky whisky, cream and raspberries, so I've added a little chocolate (what else?) and piled cranachan on top of pavlova to go all out, over the top, everything in one, luscious and vulgar – it's a pavlova-dose! You will love it, trust me…

Meringue
6 large egg whites
a pinch of salt
350 g/1¾ cups caster/
granulated sugar
1 teaspoon pure vanilla
extract
1 teaspoon white wine
vinegar
1 teaspoon cornflour/
cornstarch
2 tablespoons cocoa
powder
¼ teaspoon ground
cinnamon
1 tablespoon cocoa nibs
(optional)

Caramelized oats
75 g/1 cup rolled oats
50 g/¼ cup caster/
granulated sugar

Whisky chantilly cream
500 ml/2 cups double/
heavy cream
1–2 tablespoons icing/
confectioners' sugar
2 tablespoons Grue de
Cacao whisky (see page
158) or whisky

To assemble
400–500 g/4–5 cups
raspberries
chocolate sauce
(see page 124)

2 large baking sheets,
greased and lined with
baking parchment

Serves 6–8

Preheat the oven to 200°C (400°F) Gas 6.

Draw a 20-cm/8-inch circle on each baking sheet using a cake pan as a guide. Flip the baking parchment over so that the circle is visible through the paper but the pen or pencil marks are face-down.

To make the meringue, whisk the egg whites with the salt in a stand mixer until they hold stiff peaks but are not dry. Add the sugar 1 tablespoon at a time, mixing well between each addition so that the sugar completely dissolves before you add another tablespoon. Once all of the sugar has been added, whisk in the vanilla followed by the vinegar and cornflour/cornstarch until combined.

Scoop half of the meringue (weigh it for accuracy) into a clean bowl and sift over half of the cocoa powder and ground cinnamon. Very gently fold, no more than one or two strokes using a large metal spoon, then scoop the meringue onto one of the prepared baking sheets. Using a palette knife very carefully spread the meringue to fill the circle that you've drawn. Repeat with the remaining meringue, cocoa powder and ground cinnamon. Scatter the tops of the meringues with cocoa nibs (if using) and place on the middle shelves of the preheated oven.

Immediately reduce the heat to 120°C (250°F) Gas ½ and bake for 45 minutes. After this time, turn the sheets around, swap them over on the shelves and continue to cook for another 45 minutes–1 hour. Turn the oven off and leave the meringues inside to cool completely.

To make the caramelized oats, combine the oats and sugar in a heavy-bottomed frying pan/skillet set over a low–medium heat, stirring constantly for about 5 minutes until the oats become crisp and are coated in golden caramel. Transfer to a sheet of non-stick baking parchment and set aside to cool.

Meanwhile, whip the cream with the icing/confectioners' sugar and whisky until it holds luscious, floppy peaks.

To assemble, place one of the meringues on a serving plate and top with half of the whisky chantilly cream. Scatter with half of the raspberries and a handful of caramelized oats. Top with the second meringue, then the remaining whisky chantilly cream, raspberries and caramelized oats.

To finish, drizzle with chocolate sauce and serve soon after assembling as the cream will soften the meringue layers.

Dark chocolate panna cotta with cherry compote

My girlfriend is dairy- and wheat-intolerant, so it's often a challenge to cook and create desserts for her – a challenge I am more than happy to accept of course! Last year I took her to Luke's Dining Room, where my mate and chef patron Luke Thomas prepared her a delicious panna cotta made with soya milk and with a cherry compote on top. We owe thanks to Luke, as this is now one of her favourites! I've added chocolate and hazelnut milk here and crushed some hazelnut nougatine on top for extra bite.

Panna cotta
250 g/2 cups dark/ bittersweet chocolate (70%), finely chopped
7 leaves platinum-grade gelatine
800 ml/3⅓ cups hazelnut or soy milk
100 g/½ cup golden caster/granulated sugar
1 vanilla pod/bean, split
a pinch of salt

Cherry compote
350 g/3½ cups fresh or frozen dark cherries
3 tablespoons golden caster/granulated sugar
2 tablespoons ruby port
1 strip orange zest
½ vanilla pod/bean, split

Hazelnut nougatine
150 g/¾ cup caster/granulated sugar
100 g/1½ cups roasted hazelnuts

8 x 175-ml/6-oz. capacity ramekins or dariole moulds, lightly greased with sunflower oil

Serves 8

To make the panna cotta, put the chopped chocolate into a heatproof bowl and set aside.

In a separate bowl, soak the gelatine leaves in cold water for 10 minutes to soften.

Put the hazelnut milk, sugar, vanilla and salt in a saucepan or pot set over a medium heat, until just boiling. Pour the hot cream over the chopped chocolate and whisk until velvety smooth and the chocolate has completely melted into the milk. Drain the gelatine, blot briefly on a paper towel to remove any excess water and add it to the chocolately milk. Whisk until melted and thoroughly incorporated.

Divide the mixture between the ramekins and let cool. Cover with clingfilm/plastic wrap and chill in the fridge for at least 4 hours, until set.

To make the cherry compote, tip all of the ingredients into a saucepan or pot set over a low–medium heat and cook until it thickens.

Remove the orange zest and vanilla pod and set aside to cool.

To make the hazelnut nougatine, tip the sugar into a small heavy-bottomed frying pan/skillet set over a low–medium heat. Add 1 tablespoon of water and dissolve the sugar without stirring. Bring to the boil and continue to cook until the sugar becomes an amber-coloured caramel. Swirl the pan if necessary to ensure the caramel cooks evenly. Add the roasted hazelnuts, stir to coat the nuts in the caramel and turn out onto a sheet of non-stick baking parchment. Let cool completely before blitzing in a food processor or crushing with a rolling pin to a coarse crumb.

To serve, quickly dip the ramekins, one at a time, into a bowl of hot water and turn the panna cotta out onto serving plates. Serve with a good spoonful of cherry compote and a sprinkling of hazelnut nougatine on top.

White chocolate, coconut rice pudding with caramelized mango

Caramelized coconut
1 coconut
**1 tablespoon icing/
   confectioners' sugar**

Rice pudding
**150 g/¾ cup pudding
   or short-grain rice**
**50 g/¼ cup golden caster/
   granulated sugar**
**2 fresh or dried kaffir lime
   leaves**
**2 cardamom pods, lightly
   crushed**
a pinch of salt
**400 ml/1⅔ cups semi-
   skimmed/skim milk**
**350 ml/1½ cups coconut
   milk**
**125 g/1 cup white
   chocolate, chopped**

Mango compote
**125 g/½ cup plus
   2 tablespoons caster/
   granulated sugar**
**2 mangoes, peeled, stone/
   pit removed and sliced**
**½ teaspoon dried pink
   peppercorns, lightly
   crushed**
**freshly squeezed juice and
   grated zest of 1 lime**

*a baking sheet, greased
   and lined with baking
   parchment*

Serves 6

When I was young and a little under the weather, I'd be given canned rice pudding with a splodge of jam in the middle. This unctuous white chocolate rice pudding, made with coconut milk and infused with kaffir lime leaves, is so full of flavour it's bound to make you feel better and if that doesn't do the trick the caramelized coconut will do the trick – the stuff is addictive.

Preheat the oven to 170°C (325°C) Gas 3.

Begin by preparing the caramelized coconut. Crack open the coconut, drain the coconut water into a jug/pitcher and using a vegetable peeler to cut the flesh into fine strips. Spread the coconut on the prepared baking sheet and dust with icing/confectioners' sugar. Bake on the middle shelf for 3–4 minutes until golden and starting to caramelize. Remove from the oven and set aside to cool.

To make the rice pudding, put the rice in a fine sieve/strainer and rinse under cold running water for 3 minutes to get rid of any starch. Transfer the drained rice to a heavy-bottomed saucepan or pot, add 50 g/¼ cup of the sugar, the kaffir lime leaves, crushed cardamom pods and salt. Add 300 ml/1¼ cups of the semi-skimmed/skim milk and bring to the boil, stirring occasionally. Reduce the heat and gently simmer until almost all of the milk has been absorbed.

Gradually add the remaining semi-skimmed/skim milk and coconut milk, stirring frequently. When almost all of the milk has been absorbed and the rice is tender, remove the pan from the heat. Take out the kaffir lime leaves and cardamom pods, add the chopped white chocolate and stir to melt.

To make the mango compote, tip the sugar into a small heavy-bottomed frying pan/skillet set over a low–medium heat. Add 1 tablespoon of water and dissolve the sugar without stirring. Bring to the boil and continue to cook until the sugar becomes an amber-coloured caramel. Swirl the pan if necessary to ensure the caramel cooks evenly. Add the sliced mangoes, peppercorns and lime juice and zest. Cook until the mango has softened and infused with the lime and spice.

Serve the rice pudding in small glass bowls with the mango compote on top, garnished with caramelized coconut.

Roasted fig, walnut & chocolate pizza

In the last couple of years, I've worked with some top producers and brands to create some chocolatey twists on ingredients and drinks, including cacao olive oil and roasted cacao and vanilla beer. Both seemed impossible, but the end results were delicious. It can be the same with any recipe; sometimes you've just got to go for it and try the unimaginable. I wanted to make a chocolate pizza that could be served anytime, anywhere and to anyone. Here, a pizza dough is topped with chocolate frangipane and finished with creamy mascarpone cheese, ripe figs, crunchy walnuts, fragrant lemon thyme and a drizzle of honey. It makes the perfect end to an Italian meal or any meal infact, it's just gorgeous!

Dough
- **5 g/1 teaspoon active dry yeast**
- **a large pinch of caster/granulated sugar**
- **450–500 g/3⅓–4 cups strong white bread flour, plus a little extra for dusting**
- **2 tablespoons fruity extra virgin olive oil**
- **a large pinch of salt**

Chocolate frangipane
- **25 g/2 tablespoons grated dark/bittersweet chocolate**
- **50 g/3½ tablespoons unsalted butter, softened**
- **50 g/¼ cup caster/granulated sugar**
- **2 eggs, lightly beaten**
- **50 g/½ cup ground almonds**
- **1 tablespoon plain/all-purpose flour**
- **2 teaspoons cocoa powder**
- **a pinch of salt**

To assemble
- **8 fresh figs, quartered**
- **100 g/1 cup walnuts, roughly chopped**
- **200 g/1 cup mascarpone or ricotta**
- **3–4 tablespoons clear fragrant honey**
- **lemon thyme, to serve**

2 large baking sheets, greased and lined with baking parchment

Makes 10 slices

Measure 300 ml/1¼ cups hot water into a mixing bowl. Add the yeast and sugar, and whisk well to dissolve the yeast. Set in a warm place for 5 minutes, or until the yeast has formed a light froth on top of the liquid.

Add 450 g/3⅓ cups of flour, the olive oil and salt to the yeasty liquid and mix until it forms a rough dough, adding more flour if needed. Turn the dough out onto a lightly floured surface and knead for at least 5 minutes until the dough is smooth and elastic.

Bring the dough together and form a ball with your hands. Place in a lightly oiled mixing bowl, cover with clingfilm/plastic wrap and set in a warm, dark place for at least 1 hour, or until the dough has doubled or trebled in size. You can also prove the dough in the fridge overnight, but bring it back to room temperature before rolling out.

While the dough is proving, prepare the chocolate frangipane. Melt the chocolate in a heatproof bowl set over a saucepan or pot of simmering water. Stir until smooth and let cool slightly.

Preheat the oven to 220°C (425°F) Gas 7.

Cream the butter and sugar together until pale and light. Gradually add the beaten eggs, mixing well between each addition. Then add the ground almonds, flour, cocoa powder and salt, and mix until smooth. Add the melted chocolate and mix again.

Turn out the proved dough onto a lightly floured surface and knead gently for 1 minute to knock out any air pockets. Cut the dough in half, roll each piece out to a rough round shape about 3 mm/⅛ inch thick and arrange on the prepared baking sheets.

Spread the pizzas with the chocolate frangipane, leaving a border of about 1 cm/⅜ inch around the edge. Arrange the figs and walnuts on top and dot teaspoons of mascarpone or ricotta around the figs. Drizzle the pizzas with honey and bake on the middle shelf of the preheated oven for 10–12 minutes, until the dough is crisp, golden and risen around the edges.

Scatter lemon thyme across the pizzas, drizzle with extra honey and serve.

Brownie base

90 g/6 tablespoons unsalted butter

225 g/1²⁄₃ cups dark/bittersweet chocolate (70%), chopped

200 g/1 cup soft light brown sugar

2 eggs

1 teaspoon pure vanilla extract

a pinch of salt

70 g/generous ½ cup plain/all-purpose flour

50 g/⅓ cup blanched hazelnuts, toasted

Ganache

400 ml/1²⁄₃ cups whipping/heavy cream

20 g/1 generous tablespoon clear honey

1 teaspoon pure vanilla extract

a large pinch of salt

350 g/3 cups dark/bittersweet chocolate (70%), finely chopped

80 g/6 tablespoons unsalted butter, diced

Glaze

100 g/¾ cup dark/bittersweet chocolate

45 g/3 tablespoons unsalted butter

40 ml/3 tablespoons whole milk

15 g/1 tablespoon clear honey

To serve

cacao nibs

edible gold leaf

15 g/1 cup store-bought salted caramel popcorn

a 20 x 30-cm/8 x 12-inch baking pan, greased and lined with baking parchment

Serves 16

Jamie's 'death by chocolate' brownies

This recipe was given to me by Jamie Oliver and his pastry chef Ed Loftus. This 'death by chocolate' brownie was the dessert that beat the Italians in Channel 4's *Jamie and Jimmy's Food Fight Club*, alongside my Earl Grey sticky toffee pudding. It's an amazingly moist brownie studded with roasted hazelnuts, topped with chocolate ganache and finished with cacao nibs and caramelized popcorn! I don't know how many we made, but it certainly did the job. Thanks boys!

Preheat the oven to 170°C (325°F) Gas 3.

To make the brownie base, melt the butter and chocolate together in a heatproof bowl set over a saucepan or pot of simmering water. Stir until smooth, remove from the heat and let cool slightly. In a separate bowl, whisk together the sugar, eggs, vanilla and salt for about 5 minutes or until the mixture is pale, light and holds a firm ribbon trail when the whisk is lifted from the bowl – this is more easily achieved using a stand mixer or an electric hand whisk. Using a rubber spatula or large metal spoon, fold the chocolate and butter mixture into the eggs. Sift in the flour and gently mix until combined. Add the nuts and mix again. Pour the batter into the prepared baking pan and bake on the middle shelf of the preheated oven for 20 minutes, until the brownies are set with a light crust on top.

Remove the brownies from the oven and set aside to cool completely.

To make the ganache, tip the cream, honey, vanilla and salt into a small saucepan or pot set over a low–medium heat and bring to just below boiling point. Put the chopped chocolate into a bowl and add the hot cream, whisking constantly until melted, smooth and shiny. Add the butter and whisk to combine.

Pour the ganache over the cooled brownie base in an even layer and leave to set at room temperature for 3–4 hours.

To make the glaze, combine all of the ingredients in a small saucepan or pot set over a medium heat, and mix until smooth and shiny. Cool slightly and then pour over the ganache-topped brownie in an even layer. Set in the fridge to chill for at least 30 minutes before serving.

Using a hot, sharp knife cut the brownies into neat rectangles and position a cluster of popcorn at one end, cacao nibs in the middle and a small piece of gold leaf at the other end of each piece. For best results, bring to room temperature 1 hour before serving.

Chocolate waffles with maple syrup

Whether served as a retro dessert or an indulgent breakfast, these waffles are a real treat. Light and fluffy, drizzled with maple syrup and a scoop of vanilla ice cream, you can also use the batter to make American-style chocolate pancakes. Caramelized white chocolate finishes this dish – it's easy to do, so do it!

150 g/1¼ cups white chocolate, chopped
200 g/1⅔ cups plain/all-purpose flour
50 g/¼ cup caster/granulated sugar
1 tablespoon cocoa powder
1½ teaspoons baking powder
½ teaspoon bicarbonate of/baking soda
a large pinch of salt
3 eggs, separated
1 teaspoon pure vanilla extract
300 ml/1¼ cups buttermilk, at room temperature
50 g/3½ tablespoons unsalted butter
100 g/¾ cup dark/bittersweet chocolate, finely chopped
sunflower oil spray, for greasing the waffle iron

To serve
vanilla or chocolate ice cream
maple syrup

a small baking sheet, greased and lined with baking parchment
a waffle iron

Makes 6 waffles

Preheat the oven to 170°C (325°F) Gas 3.

Start by making the caramelized white chocolate. Tip the chopped chocolate onto the prepared baking sheet and bake in the preheated oven for 5 minutes. Using a rubber spatula, scoop the melted chocolate into a mixing bowl and beat until smooth. Return to the parchment-covered sheet and heat in the oven for a further 5 minutes. Beat the mixture again, return to the oven and continue this cooking and beating pattern until the chocolate becomes fudge-coloured – this can take up to 30 minutes. Spread onto a clean sheet of baking parchment and set aside until cold and set firm.

Preheat the waffle iron according to the manufacturer's instructions.

To make the waffles, sift the flour, sugar, cocoa powder, baking powder, bicarbonate of/baking soda and salt into a large mixing bowl. In a separate bowl, beat together the egg yolks, vanilla and buttermilk.

Melt the butter and half of the dark/bittersweet chocolate in a heatproof bowl set over a small saucepan or pot of simmering water. Stir until smooth and set aside to cool.

Make a well in the middle of the sifted dry ingredients, add the buttermilk mixture and melted chocolate and butter mixture and whisk until smooth. In another bowl whisk the egg whites until they hold stiff peaks and, using a large metal spoon, fold into the batter along with the remaining chopped chocolate.

Cook the batter in the waffle iron according to the manufacturer's instructions and serve with scoops of ice cream and maple syrup. Crumble the caramelized white chocolate over the top for an extra chocolate hit.

Drinks & ice creams

Aztec hot chocolate

Cacao was discovered by the Aztecs and was often referred to as the 'food of the gods' because of its richness and health benefits. The cacao was placed in a sort of pestle and mortar and ground with chilli, other spices and hot water added to make a drink. You can of course use normal chilli powder, but if you want something more smoky then use a chipotle chilli powder.

2 tablespoons light brown sugar, clear honey or agave syrup
1 cinnamon stick
1 teaspoon pure vanilla extract or ½ vanilla pod/bean
3 cardamom pods, lightly bruised
1 strip orange peel
½–1 teaspoon chilli powder
freshly grated nutmeg
200 g/1½ cups dark/bittersweet chocolate (70%), finely chopped
ground cinnamon, to serve

Serves 4

Pour 500 ml/2 cups of water into a saucepan or pot set over a low heat. Add the sugar, cinnamon stick, vanilla, cardamom pods, orange peel, chilli powder and nutmeg. Bring to a gentle simmer, then remove from the heat and set aside for 30 minutes to allow the spices to fully infuse with the water.

Remove the whole spices and orange peel and discard. Add the chopped chocolate to the pan and reheat to just below boiling point, stirring constantly to smoothly melt the chocolate. I like to whizz the hot chocolate using a handheld mixer to ensure that not only is the hot chocolate silky smooth but also has a good foam on top.

Pour the hot chocolate into cups or heatproof glasses and serve immediately with a pinch of ground cinnamon on top.

Opposite: Aztec hot chocolate; page 152 Gingerbread hot chocolate; page 153 Chocolate mountain

Gingerbread hot chocolate

When you're sitting out in the cold around a fire, wrapped in jumpers, this is the perfect warmer. It's lovely with a dash of brandy… for the adults only of course! Or to jazz it up for the kids try the Chocolate Mountain variation, which features copious amounts of whipped cream, marshmallows and flaked chocolate on top.

1 litre/4 cups whole milk
3 tablespoons ginger or gingerbread syrup
1 cinnamon stick
2 whole cloves
2–3 strips orange peel
2 tablespoons brandy or orange-flavoured liqueur (optional)
450 g/3¾ cups dark/bittersweet chocolate, chopped

Makes 4–6

Chocolate Mountain
300 ml/1¼ cups double/heavy cream
1 teaspoon pure vanilla extract
½ teaspoon ground cinnamon
freshly grated nutmeg, to serve
a large handful mini marshmallows
4–6 flaked chocolate bars

a large piping/pastry bag fitted with a large star nozzle/tip

Makes 4–6

Pour the milk into a saucepan or pot set over a medium heat. Add the ginger syrup, cinnamon stick, cloves, orange peel and brandy (if using) and bring slowly to the boil, stirring occasionally to allow the spices to infuse with the milk.

Meanwhile tip the chopped chocolate into a large jug/pitcher. Pour the hot, spice-infused milk onto the chocolate and whisk until silky smooth. Strain into cups and serve.

To make a Chocolate Mountain, whip the cream with the vanilla and ground cinnamon until it will hold a soft peak. Scoop the cream into a piping/pastry bag fitted with a large star nozzle/tip. Pipe generous swirls of whipped cream on top of each hot chocolate. Top the cream with freshly grated nutmeg, scatter with marshmallows and add a flaked chocolate bar to finish.

Mango, passion fruit & white chocolate milkshake

When a friend got married last year, we went to an American-style bowling alley in London where after the bowling we gorged ourselves on Southern fried chicken and all had milkshakes. The tropical flavours of mango and passion fruit work incredibly well with white chocolate when whizzed up in a food processor with some ice cream – it's really refreshing yet indulgent at the same time!

2 ripe mangoes, peeled and stone/pit removed
3 large passion fruit
500 ml/2 cups whole milk
5 large scoops white chocolate ice cream

Variations (see right)
3 limes
1 teaspoon yuzu juice
100 g/1 cup raspberries
5 scoops dark/bittersweet chocolate ice cream
5 scoops milk/semisweet ice cream
200 g/2 cups raspberries
170 g/1½ cups smooth peanut butter

Serves 2

Place the mango flesh into a food processor or blender and set aside.

Halve two of the passion fruit and scoop the juice, flesh and seeds into a sieve/strainer set over the food processor. Push the pulp through the sieve/strainer and discard the seeds. Blend the mango and passion fruit together until smooth.

Add the milk and ice cream and blend again until the mixture is smooth and creamy. Pour into two tall glasses and serve with the seeds and pulp of the remaining passion fruit over the top.

Variations

For a tangier variation of this milkshake, keep the white chocolate ice cream and the passion fruit, but remove one of the mangoes. Add the juice of 3 limes and a teaspoon of yuzu juice to the food processor before the final blending and serve as above.

For a dark/bittersweet chocolate berry milkshake, replace the mango and passion fruit with raspberries and add dark/bittersweet chocolate ice cream instead of white and prepare as before.

For a peanut butter, raspberry and chocolate milkshake, use milk/semisweet chocolate ice cream, lots of fresh raspberries and smooth peanut butter – you'll never go back!

Chocolate mulled wine

This is the most decadent hot chocolate you will ever have and the most indulgent mulled wine at the same time. I've used a really fruity chocolate from the Dominican Republic, where the cocoa has a natural red fruit undertone to it that works really well the richness of the red wine, port and spices. I served this at a Christmas Eve party one year and it all went in seconds – people loved it!

750 ml/3 cups red wine
2 cinnamon sticks
6 cloves
2 star anise
1 large sprig fresh rosemary
2 bay leaves
4 cardamom pods
½ vanilla pod/bean
1 orange, sliced
200 g/1 cup soft light brown
250 g/2 cups fruity dark/
**   bittersweet chocolate**
**   (I use Saint-Domingue from**
**   Cacao Barry)**
2 tablespoons ruby port,
**   optional**

Serves 4–6

Pour the red wine into a saucepan or pot set over a low heat. Add the cinnamon sticks, cloves, star anise, rosemary and bay leaves.

Lightly bruise the cardamom pods and add them, along with the half a vanilla pod/bean, to the pan with the orange slices. Add the sugar and slowly heat the wine, taking care not to let it boil.

Remove the pan from the heat and set aside for 30 minutes to allow the spices to fully infuse with the wine.

Add the chopped chocolate to the pan and reheat to just below boiling point, stirring constantly to smoothly melt the chocolate. Add the port (if using), mix again and strain into heatproof glasses to serve.

Opposite: Chocolate mulled wine

Chocolate tea

Adding roasted cacao nibs to loose tea really changes its flavour and adds a delicate bitterness. Avoid light-bodied and delicate teas such as Earl Grey as the cacao will take over. For me, Assam tea works well, because of its malty, bold and full-bodied flavour. The nibs also give the tea a wonderfully dark, bourbon colour. Add the cacao nibs to loose-leaf tea in a pot to allow the flavours to infuse – you won't achieve the same taste with a tea bag!

3–4 teaspoons Assam tea
**   leaves or other tea of your**
**   choice**
1 teaspoon cacao nibs
sugar or honey, to taste

Serves 2–4

Begin by warming the tea pot by carefully swirling a small amount of hot water in it.

Add the tea leaves and cacao nibs then pour in the boiling water. Stir and leave to brew for 3–4 minutes. Sweeten with sugar or honey and serve.

Note
If you want a stronger chocolate flavour, just add more cacao nibs while the tea is in the pot, and leave to infuse.

Chocolate Irish coffee

When I was younger and we visited my Nans and Pops in the Cotswold town of Stroud, we would always walk into the town centre to have a drink in the Imperial Hotel. My sister and I would each get a magazine and a fizzy drink, while my parents and my Nans would have an Irish coffee; I always wondered how they got the cream to sit on top without it sinking. Adding the chocolate-infused Roasted Grué de Cacao Whisky to coffee makes for the perfect after dinner tipple.

coffee and cocoa powder,
  for dusting
250 ml/1 cup freshly brewed
  coffee
1 tablespoon demerara/
  turbinado sugar

2 tablespoon Roasted Grué
  de Cacao Whisky (right)
250 ml/1 cup double/ heavy
  cream

Serves 1

The first thing I remember being told about making the perfect Irish coffee is to use a tall, warm glass. Pour boiling water from a kettle into the glass and then pour it away.

You could at this point swirl some coffee and cocoa powder around the inside of the glass to make it even more indulgent and chocolatey.

Pour in the freshly brewed coffee leaving a gap at the top. Stir in the demerara/turbinado sugar and the whisky.

Pour the double/heavy cream over the back of a teaspoon near one side of the glass and let it float on top. Dust with a little extra cocoa powder and enjoy.

Roasted grué de cacao whisky

The smokiness of whisky is comparable to that of gently roasted cocoa nibs, and so if you like whisky and you love chocolate, this is the drink for you. It will take your whisky drinking to a whole new level.

50 g/²⁄₃ cup cacao nibs
500 ml/2 cups whisky

Makes 550 ml/2²⁄₃ cups
and serves 8–10

Preheat the oven to 180°C (350°F) Gas 4.

Tip the cocoa nibs into a small roasting pan and roast in the preheated oven for about 4 minutes, or until you can smell their aroma.

Meanwhile, gently heat the whisky in a small saucepan or pot set over a low heat until hot but not boiling.

Pour the hot whisky into a sterilized glass jar, add the roasted cacao nibs and leave until cold before sealing with an airtight lid. Shake the bottle a couple of times and leave in a cool, dark place for at least a week before using. Shake the jar once a day to further infuse the whisky. Serve straight, over ice.

Note
This infused whisky will keep for several weeks – the flavour becoming more pronounced the longer it is kept. This method of infusing the roasted cacao nibs into hot alcohol works really well with other liqueurs and spirits too. Amaretto di Saronno and Grand Marnier are my two favourites!

Opposite: Roasted grué de cacao whisky

White chocolate, orange & cinnamon sorbet

This is a light and refreshing dessert that is gently spiced with cinnamon and enriched with orange liqueur. I like to top it with a spoonful of very simple candied orange – the perfect alternative to a heavy dessert for a dinner party.

Sorbet
175 g/¾ cup caster/ granulated sugar
2 teaspoons ground cinnamon
freshly squeezed juice and finely grated zest of 2 small mandarins or 1 orange
seeds of ½ vanilla pod/ bean
2 tablespoons Grand Marnier or other orange liqueur
200 g/1½ cups white chocolate, chopped

Candied orange zest
2 oranges, peeled
400 g/2 cups caster/ granulated sugar

an ice cream machine

Makes 1½ litres/2½ pints and serves 8–10

Begin by making the sorbet syrup base. Tip the sugar into a saucepan or pot set over a low heat. Add 350 ml/1⅓ cup of water and heat slowly to dissolve the sugar. Add the cinnamon, mandarin juice and grated zest as well as the vanilla and bring to the boil. Simmer for 30 seconds, then remove from the heat. Add the Grand Marnier and set aside.

Tip the chopped chocolate into a bowl, add one third of the syrup and whisk until smooth. Add the remaining syrup and whisk again. Set aside to cool, then chill in the fridge for no more than 20 minutes while you prepare the ice cream machine according to the manufacturer's instructions. Take care not to over chill the mixture as the chocolate will set firm. Pour the sorbet mixture into the ice cream machine and churn following the manufacturer's instructions.

Scoop the frozen sorbet into a plastic box and freeze for at least 1 hour before serving.

Meanwhile, prepare the candied orange zest. Using a sharp knife cut the peel into very fine shreds. **(A)**

Tip 100 g/½ cup of the sugar into a small saucepan or pot set over a medium heat. Add 100 ml/⅓ cup of water and bring to the boil. Then add the orange shreds and simmer for 5 minutes. **(B)**

Strain the contents of the pan, discarding the syrup, and rinse the zest strips with cold running water. Return the zest strips to the pan and add a further 100 g/½ cup of sugar and 100 ml/⅓ cup of water and repeat as above. Repeat this process twice more, but do not discard the syrup the last time. **(C)**

Pour the candied zest strips with their syrup into an airtight container and set aside to cool.

Serve the sorbet in scoops, topped with candied orange zest and drizzled with syrup.

Chocolate fudge ice cream

350 ml/1⅓ cups whole milk

500 ml/2 cups double/ heavy cream

5 egg yolks

125 g/1¼ cups soft light brown sugar

150 g/1½ cups caster/ granulated sugar

2 teaspoons pure vanilla extract

a pinch of salt

40 g/⅓ cup cocoa powder

125 g/1 cup dark/ bittersweet chocolate (70%), chopped

Fudge ripple

175 ml/⅔ cup double/ heavy cream

75 g/¾ cup soft light brown sugar

4 tablespoons golden/ light corn syrup or liquid glucose

100 g/¾ cup dark/ bittersweet chocolate

30 g/¼ cup cocoa powder

25 g/2 tablespoons unsalted butter

1 teaspoon pure vanilla extract

a pinch of salt

Waffle cones

6–8 waffle cones

100 g/¾ cup tempered dark/bittersweet chocolate

chopped hazelnuts

an ice cream machine

Makes 1½ litres/2½ pints and serves 6–8

What's better, more simple and spectacular than rich chocolate fudge ice cream? I love it and have been known to eat a whole tub in front of a movie, under a blanket in the winter. Rippled with a simple fudge sauce, this chocolate ice cream is super indulgent, but isn't that what you want? It was made to make you smile! The crunch of ice cream cones reminds me of summer holidays too, so I've just dipped the top in some chocolate and chopped nuts to add an extra textural dimension.

To make the ice cream, heat the milk and half of the cream in a saucepan or pot set over a medium heat until just below boiling.

Meanwhile, whisk together the egg yolks, both sugars, vanilla and salt in a large mixing bowl until smooth and light.

Steadily pour 3–4 tablespoons of the hot milk into the egg mixture, whisking constantly until smooth. Add the cocoa powder and whisk again. Add the remaining milk and whisk until combined. Return the mixture to the pan and cook over a low heat, stirring constantly, for about 3 minutes, or until the mixture thickens enough to coat the back of a spoon. Take care not to let it boil or the eggs will scramble.

Tip the chopped chocolate into a large mixing bowl and pour the hot mixture on top. Add the remaining double/heavy cream and whisk until you have a silky smooth, chocolatey custard. Set aside until cool, then cover with clingfilm/plastic wrap and chill in the fridge for at least 1 hour.

Meanwhile, prepare the fudge ripple. Put all of the ingredients in a saucepan or pot set over a low heat, and warm through, whisking constantly until smooth. Remove from the heat and cool to room temperature.

Churn in the ice cream machine according to the manufacturer's instructions. Spoon a quarter of the ice cream into a freezer container in an even layer. Top with a couple of tablespoons of fudge ripple and continue this layering, ending with a swirled layer of fudge ripple on the top. Freeze the ice cream overnight, until firm.

To serve, dip each waffle cone in tempered dark/bittersweet chocolate and then in the chopped hazelnuts. Scoop the ice cream into the cone and enjoy!

Caramelized coffee & chocolate ice cream

Served in the *affogato* style, by pouring over a hot espresso, this is the dessert for true coffee lovers. Often just served with a scoop of vanilla ice cream, I thought I'd take it to the next level by making it with chocolate and coffee ice cream. What's more, I love crunchy bits in ice cream too, so I caramelized some coffee beans and folded them through the ice cream to add texture and to release a burst of intense coffee flavour.

300 ml/1¼ cups whole milk

1 vanilla pod/bean, split

4 tablespoons coffee beans

175 g/1⅓ cups dark/bittersweet chocolate, chopped

175 g/1¾ cups caster/granulated sugar, plus extra for the coffee beans

6 egg yolks

500 ml/2 cups double/heavy cream

espresso coffee, to serve

an ice cream machine

Makes 1½ litres/2½ pints and serves 6–8

Pour the milk into a saucepan or pot set over a low heat. Add the split vanilla pod/bean and half of the coffee beans, and bring slowly to the boil. Remove from the heat and set aside to infuse for at least 2 hours, preferably longer.

Put the chocolate in a heatproof bowl set over a pan of barely simmering water. Stir until melted and smooth, and remove from the heat.

In a separate bowl, whisk together the sugar and egg yolks until pale and light. Reheat the coffee-infused milk until just below boiling and pour over the egg mixture, whisking constantly until smooth.

Pour the mixture into a clean saucepan or pot set over a low–medium heat, stirring all the time until it thickens and will coat the back of a spoon. Strain a little of the mixture over the melted chocolate, whisking constantly, and then gradually add the remaining mixture in a slow, steady stream. Mix until smooth,

then add the cream and whisk until combined. Set aside to cool, then cover and chill in the fridge for at least 2 hours before churning in the ice cream machine according to the manufacturer's instructions. Scoop the ice cream into a plastic freezer box and place in the freezer.

Meanwhile, tip the remaining coffee beans and 2 tablespoons of caster/granulated sugar into a small frying pan/skillet set over a medium heat. Stir constantly until the beans begin to release their aroma and the sugar starts to caramelize. Tip onto a sheet of baking parchment and leave to harden and cool.

Pour the cooled candied coffee beans into a food processor and whizz until the beans are roughly chopped. Stir the chopped beans through the ice cream and freeze until firm.

Serve the ice cream scooped into small cups or glass bowls with a shot of hot espresso poured over the top.

Pistachio stracciatella gelato

There is a very famous, award-winning gelateria called Jannetta's in St Andrews, Scotland, that serves some of the best ice creams ever! It's well worth a visit if you are ever in that neck of the woods; one of my favourite flavours has to be pistachio. It's just so gorgeous and delicious, but can be hard to find and tricky to get the balance of flavour right. I like to whisk melted chocolate into the ice cream before placing it in the freezer to give a texture similar to mint choc chip. Little crunchy strands of chocolate work perfectly against the beautiful pistachio flavour.

200 g/1 cup caster/ granulated sugar
6 large egg yolks
700 ml/2¾ cups whole milk
½ vanilla pod/bean, split
250 ml/1 cup double/ heavy cream
200 g/1 cup pistachio paste (available online)
a pinch of salt
100 g/¾ cup nibbed pistachios
150 g/1¼ cups dark/ bittersweet chocolate, grated

an ice cream machine

Makes 1½ litres/2½ pints and serves 6–8

To make the gelato, whisk together the sugar and egg yolks in a large mixing bowl until pale and light.

Put the milk and split vanilla pod/bean in a large saucepan or pot set over a medium heat and bring to the boil.

Slowly pour the hot milk over the egg mixture, whisking constantly until smooth. Return the mixture to the pan, place over a low–medium heat and, stirring constantly, cook the mixture for 5–7 minutes or until it will coat the back of a wooden spoon.

Remove the mixture from the heat, strain over a clean bowl and whisk in the cream, pistachio paste and salt. Set aside to cool, then cover and chill for at least 4 hours.

Churn the mixture in the ice cream machine according to the manufacturer's instructions. Scoop the gelato into a plastic freezer box and fold through three quarters of the nibbed pistachios and all of the grated chocolate until evenly distributed. Cover and freeze until firm.

Serve generous scoops of the gelato sprinkled with the remaining nibbed pistachios.

Index

Resources

You can now buy a wide range of chocolate bars from your favourite supermarket to make the most of my recipes in this book, but to help you become the Master Chocolatier, I've listed the suppliers, products and brands that I work with to help you on your way.

CHOCOLATE

Cacao Barry & Callebaut
www.cacao-barry.com
www.callebaut.com
All the recipes in this book have been designed and developed using Cacao Barry chocolate which is available, alongside products from their sister company Callebaut, at their websites. Also available to buy are decorations, truffle spheres, chocolate-making equipment and packaging.

Chocolate Trading Company
www.chocolatetradingco.com
Specialists in luxury chocolate selling gourmet gifts, bars, ingredients and decorations online for both UK and international delivery.

Home Chocolate Factory
www.homechocolatefactory.com
On-line sellers of specialist equipment for chocolatiers including a wide range of ingredients such as freeze-dried fruits, couverture, shells and transfer sheets, as well as moulds and packaging.

Keylink
www.keylink.org
'One-stop shop for everyone working with chocolate'. A wide range of ingredients, decorations, equipment and packaging.

House of Sarunds
www.sarunds.co.uk
Confectionery specialists – importers, wholesalers and distributors of luxury continental chocolate brands.

OTHER SPECIALIST INGREDIENTS

Billington's
www.billingtons.co.uk
Quality sugar products available to buy from food halls and supermarkets.

Nielsen Massey
www.nielsenmassey.com
Illinois-based manufacturers of pure vanilla extracts and other food flavourings from peppermint to rosewater.

Sous Chef
www.souschef.co.uk
Innovative on-line shop for a wide range of specialist cook's ingredients.

Amazon
www.amazon.co.uk
www.amazon.com
Useful on-line marketplace for hard-to-find ingredients

Waitrose
www.waitrose.com
Stores across the UK and stockists of a wide range of baking ingredients and other quality food products.

BAKING AND GENERAL KITCHEN EQUIPMENT

Continental Chef Supplies
www.chefs.net
Suppliers of catering equipment and clothing including dessert frames, chocolate moulds and other specialist baking equipment.

The Pampered Chef
www.pamperedchef.co.uk
www.pamperedchef.com
Direct seller of innovative kitchen tools, available through a network of Pampered Chef Consultants throughout the UK, USA and Canada.

Lakeland Ltd
www.lakeland.co.uk
'The home of creative kitchenware' and stockists of a wide range of baking equipment such as cake pans, spatulas, chocolate moulds and other useful equipment.

Thermapen
www.thermapen.co.uk
An indispensable tool for measuring precise temperatures when baking and working with chocolate.

KitchenAid
www.kitchenaid.co.uk
Premium kitchen appliances including the iconic stand mixer. Available from all good homeware stores including John Lewis in the UK and Crate & Barrel in the US.

CHEF'S CLOTHING AND APRONS

Oliver Harvey
www.oliverharvey.co.uk
British producer of tailored chef's clothing, designed to withstand the rigours of a professional kitchen.

TUTORIALS AND INSPIRATION

The Chocolate Academy™
www.chocolate-academy.com
Teaching and training centres around the globe for artisans and professionals who want to improve their skills in chocolate and learn about new trends, techniques and recipes.

Academy of Chocolate
www.academyofchocolate.org.uk
Founded in 2005 by five of Britain's leading chocolate professionals, united in the belief that eating fine chocolate is one of life's great pleasures. Members meet to taste, discuss, demonstrate and debate issues regarding the journey from bean to bar.

Acknowledgements

Firstly a massive thank you to everyone who bought my first book Pâtisserie at Home! You made my dreams come true.

This, my second book, has been an absolute joy to work on, write, design, live, breath and eat! Massive thanks to the superb team at Ryland, Peters and Small, mainly for letting me loose on my favourite subject; chocolate. Thank you to Cindy, Julia and Leslie for once again believing in me. Megan for being such great fun on the shoots and designing another beautiful book. To my editors, Céline and Stephanie, thanks yet again for putting up with me and holding my hand throughout. We did it!

This book wouldn't be where it is without the amazing talent of my recipe tester, developer and writer; Annie Rigg. You have been amazing throughout and really got inside my head and understood everything I was talking about. You are wonderfully superb and amazing to work with, also a true diamond. Thank you to my incredible assistant Emily Kydd who has been a rock on shoot; always keeping a calm head and knowing how to place those crumbs or spoon that sauce – you're an amazing mate and a true talent. Thanks also to Kathryn Morrisey who stepped into Emily's shoes on a few occasions. It was great to work with you again and you too are superb!

Which brings me on to the photography department. Barry Craig is one of the funniest guys I've ever met, whose jokes, photoshop genius and observations kept us going on many a stressful shoot moment. Seriously though, your talent and attention to detail is mind blowing and remember 'Where there's a Will, there's a Whey'. Jonathan Gregson, you have done it again. How you do it? I do not know, but you have managed to capture everything I hoped each dish or chocolate to be, all with the click of a camera. Thank you so much for being a true support, amazing friend and creating a stunning book, again!

Huge thanks to Tom, Nathan and Sara, for giving this book such wonderful support and to Jamie and Ed for one truly amazing recipe! Special thanks to Yolande Stanley MCA for continually being my mentor, friend and sounding board – you inspire me all the time and once again I wouldn't be here without you. Thank you also to Professor David Foskett, his team and students at the University of West London for helping launch Pâtisserie at Home, with such success and for your continued support. Thanks also to the Academy of Chocolate, Craft Guild of Chefs and Guild of Food Writers. Thanks to all the team at Waitrose for still being amazing and putting up with me – newness with familiarity lives on!

Enormous thanks to everyone at Cacao Barry and Callebaut – Robert, Julie, Bev and all the team, you have been such a support and so generous in giving Annie and me so much chocolate! Thanks to Leynah Bruce and the guys at Billington's for keeping me sweet, KitchenAid, the amazing team at The Pampered Chef and all at Sous Chef and Thermapen.

I am still in debt to the team at Freedom Management who have continued to help run my life. Darrin, Nick, Graham and Keith. You guys are awesome and I couldn't have done it without you – thank you all so much.

There are so many friends I could thank but I have to mention Pete Gibbs. You and Joe have been such a massive support both personally and work wise. Pete, yet again you have opened my eyes to the world of chocolate, seeing as so much has changed since I interviewed you for my dissertation all those years ago. You guys are amazing and don't worry Joe, the salted caramel chocolates line didn't make it in! To all my other friends, what can I say, but thank you for supporting me, believing in me and always making sure my feet are firmly planted on the ground.

I wouldn't be anywhere without the love and support of my family. So to Mum, Dad and Sophie – thank you for still being there, always willing to try out recipe developments and for being purely brilliant – lots of love.

Three words to Francesca – I love you. Soppy I know, but couldn't resist, Ha! You're an amazing woman who makes me laugh, inspires me, understands and believes in me and keeps me grounded every day. I'm so lucky.

And finally to JC – you're still and always will be a Superstar!